Developing Children's Resilience and Mental Health

With the increased focus on providing for children's mental health, there is ever more demand for resources that will support educational settings to help children develop the skills needed to cope in today's world. This book presents nursery and school staff with a simple, jargon-free guide which offers a creative approach to supporting young children to develop their social and emotional skills throughout the academic year.

Developing Children's Resilience and Mental Health is a comprehensive programme made up of fun, practical activities in a 32-session format. Each session contains a warm-up, main learning activity, and relaxation exercise, focusing on four REAL core themes of development:

- **R**elationships
- **E**motions
- **A**wareness
- **L**earning

Each session can be carried out on a weekly basis to build a firm foundation for children's development and to help reduce issues related to social, emotional, and behavioural difficulties. With almost 100 activities in total and session-related homework tasks, this book is a vital resource for school staff and educational practitioners.

Susana Goncalves Viana is an author, a qualified Educational Psychologist, and a school and family coach. She is founder and CEO of SerutuFutures Ltd., whose work focuses on supporting children to develop their happiness and resilience. Prior to that she worked as a Specialist Educational Psychologist for 11 years at a London Local Authority. She has also worked as a teacher in the UK and Portugal.

Developing Children's Resilience and Mental Health

REAL Skills for All Aged 4–8

Susana Goncalves Viana

LONDON AND NEW YORK

First published 2019
by Routledge
2 Park Square, Milton Park, Abingdon, Oxon OX14 4RN

and by Routledge
711 Third Avenue, New York, NY 10017

Routledge is an imprint of the Taylor & Francis Group, an informa business

© 2019 Susana Goncalves Viana

The right of Susana Goncalves Viana to be identified as author of this work has been asserted by her in accordance with sections 77 and 78 of the Copyright, Designs and Patents Act 1988.

All rights reserved. No part of this book may be reprinted or reproduced or utilised in any form or by any electronic, mechanical, or other means, now known or hereafter invented, including photocopying and recording, or in any information storage or retrieval system, without permission in writing from the publishers.

Trademark notice: Product or corporate names may be trademarks or registered trademarks, and are used only for identification and explanation without intent to infringe.

British Library Cataloguing in Publication Data
A catalogue record for this book is available from the British Library

Library of Congress Cataloging in Publication Data
A catalog record has been requested for this book

ISBN: 978-1-138-33542-4 (hbk)
ISBN: 978-1-138-33543-1 (pbk)
ISBN: 978-0-429-44379-4 (ebk)

Typeset in Helvatica
by Sunrise Setting Ltd., Brixham, UK

Dedication

To all the teachers, the learners,
The midnight-oil-burners,
The ones who go the extra mile,
And help kids grow all the while,
You're the ones who that difference make,
To always give and never take,
This book is dedicated to you,
Thank you for all that you do.

Contents

Section 1 — Introduction   **1**

Why do we need this book? 1
What is different about this programme? 2
What is this programme all about? 2
Learning objectives 3
What are the sessions like? 4
How do the children settle into the group? 5
Will we be working with parents? 5
Can I measure a child's progress? 6

Section 2 — Top tips for teachers   **7**

Working with parents 7
Working with children with special needs 9

Section 3 — Relationships   **12**

Session 1 14
Session 2 17
Session 3 18
Session 4 20
Session 5 22
Session 6 24
Session 7 26
Session 8 28

Section 4 — Emotions   **31**

Session 1 33
Session 2 35
Session 3 37
Session 4 39
Session 5 42
Session 6 43
Session 7 45
Session 8 46

Section 5 — Awareness   50

Session 1 52
Session 2 54
Session 3 56
Session 4 58
Session 5 60
Session 6 62
Session 7 64
Session 8 66

Section 6 — Learning   69

Session 1 71
Session 2 73
Session 3 75
Session 4 77
Session 5 79
Session 6 81
Session 7 84
Session 8 86

Appendices   89

Learning Objectives Table 89
Homework Activities Table 90

Section 1 – Introduction

Why do we need this book?

Today's world can be a busy and complicated place to be, with many difficulties that affect both adults and children. As adults, we have had the time and the experience to deal with life's tricky moments, but children need to develop the skills to help them cope and thrive in a tough world. We are expecting children as young as three and four to settle in their environment, communicate appropriately, make good choices, socialise well with everyone around them, make friends, be happy and resilient, be confident, motivated and engaged, and learn! What about being able to cope with their feelings and knowing what to do when faced with tricky situations? How well can they problem-solve to find solutions and cope? It is obvious that we are expecting children to do so much, yet how many adults can do all of this successfully? If we are demanding more of children every day, are we giving them the opportunities that they need to learn how to meet these demands? With an increasing focus being placed on developing academic competence, and with a gradual decrease in opportunities for children to simply play, I don't think we are giving them the time and support that they need to enable them to develop all the vital skills for future life success.

Children need opportunities and support to develop the skills that will become the foundation for learning, communication, socialisation, and positive mental health. This support needs to happen as early as possible and, with a focus on early intervention, they should be developing these skills in their pre-school and early primary years. Children acquire the necessary skills to learn and do well at school between the ages of three and seven. At this time, they are beginning to develop their language, their memory, their concentration, and their knowledge about the world. They are also developing their strengths and their personality traits, alongside their thinking, and their social and emotional skills. All of these areas are vital for school and learning readiness, and for the development of academic ability. Effective teaching and support in these early years will build a firm foundation for successful learning, healthy relationships, and a positive attitude towards school. An early intervention programme such as 'Developing Children's Resilience and Mental Health: **REAL** Skills for All Aged 4-8' can thus enhance children's academic achievement and mental health, and their future resilience and success.

Building the necessary skills early reduces the issues related to social, behavioural and emotional difficulties. If developing these skills happens early, there will be a positive effect over time from toddlers to school-aged children, to teenagers and then adults. Developing positive and healthy skills prevents the establishment of damaging patterns within schools and families. It can break the cycle of negativity and difficulty, and build strong and positive patterns that will continue to develop and last a lifetime. This programme therefore provides a framework to enable teaching staff and parents to focus on developing children's social and emotional wellbeing, and learning behaviours, which will equip them with the necessary skills to grow and cope both inside and outside school.

What is different about this programme?

There are a number of books and programmes available that focus on helping children to develop individual areas such as building friendships, nurturing self-awareness, encouraging emotional understanding, and developing skills related to readiness for learning. However, this programme focuses on developing all of these areas because they are all vital skills that contribute to a child's overall development and ability to reach their full potential. Furthermore, the majority of books and programmes that are available to support the development of these vital skills are aimed at working with junior-aged children and teenagers, but this programme focuses on helping children in the early years. The sessions in this book aim to help nursery and school staff, and education professionals, to work with children from four to eight years of age, given that the earlier children develop these skills, the more they can build on them, and the easier things will become as they get older.

Trying to engage children in tasks where they have to sit for prolonged lengths of time to talk about themselves or their feelings, to talk through scenarios or just listen to an adult, or to try and develop skills by completing worksheets is not an effective way to help young children learn. Young children learn best by engaging in activities that are practical and creative; this comprehensive programme therefore offers a structured array of sessions that are fun and easy to understand, and even supports the development of appropriate relaxation skills.

What is this programme all about?

'Developing Children's Resilience and Mental Health: **REAL** Skills for All Aged 4–8' is a programme for children who are in later nursery and in the infant years of primary school, and will therefore work best for those aged four to eight years of age. This broad programme focuses on four core **REAL** areas:

1. **R**elationships
2. **E**motions
3. **A**wareness
4. **L**earning

This programme will therefore focus on the skills needed to build positive relationships, to be self-aware and aware of others, to recognise and express easy and difficult feelings, and to be able to learn effectively. Although there are specific learning objectives and activities related to building these core skills, there are learning skills that run throughout the programme in the way that the children engage with each session, each activity, and with each other. These are also vital skills needed for successful learning and include the following areas:

- Speaking and listening
- Turn-taking and sharing
- Concentration and focus
- Motivation and confidence
- Collaboration and cooperation

Learning objectives

Learning objectives are set out for each session around the four core areas, and the games and activities are structured around these objectives. Since this programme focuses on the early years and children aged four to eight years of age, the activities included are both visual and extremely practical to ensure that they are able to engage successfully in all of the sessions. The table that follows outlines the four core areas and their corresponding objectives for 32 sessions. The rationale behind having 32 sessions is that children can access one session a week, given that a school year is around 38 weeks long. This therefore allows a few weeks at the beginning of the year for school staff and supporting professionals to choose the children who will take part, gather the resources needed, allocate a physical space for the group to meet, and seek parental consent. Once the children complete the programme, they will then have a few weeks before the end of the academic year to evaluate their progress and have a celebration of their achievements.

I have included a copy of this 'Learning Objectives' table in the appendices; it can be photocopied and stuck in each child's homework book so that parents are aware of what the objectives are for the whole programme.

Core Area	Objective
Relationships	I know what a good friend is
	I know that I am a good friend
	I know who my friends are and why
	I know who is in my family
	I know how to make friends
	I know how to keep my friends
	I know what I like doing with my friends
	I know how to do something kind for others
Emotions	I know when I feel happy or sad
	I know when others feel happy or sad
	I know what makes me and others feel happy
	I know what makes me and others feel sad
	I know when I am feeling angry
	I know what makes me feel angry
	I know how to make myself feel better
	I know how to make others feel better
Awareness	I know things about me such as what I look like
	I know what is special about me
	I know what I like and what I don't like
	I know how we are the same and different
	I know that I can make good choices
	I know what to do if I haven't made a good choice
	I know how my choices can affect others
	I know how to show others I care about them
Learning	I know what I am good at
	I know how to use what I am good at to help me
	I know how to work in a group
	I know how to tell others when I need or want something
	I know how to ask for help
	I know how to keep going when things are hard
	I know what I want to get better at
	I know it's okay to make mistakes

What are the sessions like?

This programme has been created to be delivered in a small group of children, and works best with a group of six children or less. It consists of 32 sessions that should each last around 45 minutes. Each session consists of a settling-down poem, a warm-up game, a main activity, and a relaxation exercise. A list of resources that you will need for every session is outlined at the end of every session description. A homework task linked to the main activity is also included for each session; a copy of these homework tasks has been included in the appendices as a 'Homework Activities Table' so that adults can easily photocopy the pages, cut out the individual tasks, and stick these directly into the children's homework books at the beginning or end of every session.

It will also be important for members of staff running this programme to incorporate both team and individual rewards for the children to work towards during each session. The types of rewards should depend on the individual children and the dynamics of each group, taking into account what will work best for them (e.g. stones in a jar for teamwork, stickers for good sharing, prizes for individual achievements, etc.)

How do the children settle into the group?

When the children come together in a group, the poem outlined below will help them to recognise what time it is and to settle into the session. By repeating this poem at the beginning of each session, the children will be able to learn it over time, both in the words and the actions used. This poem will cue the children in to know when it is time to start the session. If you want, you can also have some fun music playing in the background whilst you act out the poem.

> *Here are my ears, I can hear* (with the action of touching their ears)
> *Here are my eyes, I can see* (with the action of touching their eyes)
> *Here is my heart, I can feel* (with the action of holding their hands to their heart)
> *Here is my friend, next to me* (with the action of holding hands with friends next to them)
> *I am ready to learn and play* (with the action of swinging their hands together)
> *I'm sitting down, legs crossed, hooray!* (with the action of sitting with their legs crossed)

Will we be working with parents?

The development of positive social and emotional skills, and learning and school readiness, should develop naturally with the support of caring adults in every child's life. Working with parents will thus be an important part of this programme as a positive partnership between parents and school staff will ensure greater consistency and thus the success of what the children learn. First of all, you will need to gain parental permission from parents to involve their children in the programme, and they should be informed as to the length, content, and purpose of the sessions, to enable them to give their informed consent.

Each session has a corresponding homework task that is directly linked to the main activity carried out at school. Every child taking part in the group therefore needs a homework book where tasks can be set out, and where parents can work with them at home. Homework will aim to reinforce the concepts and skills that the children are learning at school, and should ensure consistency of approach. Ideally then, homework tasks need to be done at home with parental support, but if for any reason this is difficult or not possible, then it will be important for a member of school staff to do this homework task with the child before the next session.

Can I measure a child's progress?

It will be important to measure a child's progress throughout the programme, by jointly (with the child) setting relevant targets for each individual taking part in the group. Both school staff and parents will need to think of areas that they would like the children to develop during the course of the 32 sessions. Before the start of the programme, school staff running the group will need to set two targets for each child, and parents will also need to set two targets for their children. These targets should be related to the four core areas of the programme: building positive relationships, recognising and dealing with emotions, being aware of self and others, and the foundation skills for learning.

Once parents and school staff have set two targets for each child, they then need to scale where the children are at the beginning of the programme. This can be done on a scale from one to ten, where one is the worst it has ever been and ten is the best. At the end of every session, school staff and parents need to check the targets they have set, with the child, and scale where the children are so that they are evaluating their progress across the 32 sessions.

Section 2 – Top tips for teachers

Working with parents

Research focusing on the most effective methods to support children's holistic development outlines that parental involvement in school life can be a predictor for children's school success as it helps learning to be more consistent across both home and school. This does not just have advantages for the children; schools that welcome support and active engagement from parents helps them to feel listened to, that their opinions and concerns are acknowledged and valued, and they enable them to feel that they are fully involved in their child's learning. Since children learn best through working collaboratively with the most influential adults that care for and support them on a daily basis, this includes both school staff as well as parents. Working with parents is always an opportunity to build trusting and collaborative relationships between home and school. Furthermore, we always need to be aware that by 'parent', we need to consider that this could be a single parent, a grandparent, a guardian, or even a foster carer.

All 32 of the activities in this book include a homework task so that the children can continue practising and consolidating their skills at home. In order for this to be successful, then parental involvement is an important part of this learning journey and the following therefore needs to be put in place:

- In order to let parents know about your intention to carry out this programme with the children, it will be beneficial to invite them in to school from the beginning. Meeting with parents in this way lets you share your vision with them before you start carrying out the activities with the children, and gives you the opportunity to tell parents about what you will be doing, what learning will be involved, the homework tasks that the children will be doing outside of school, and how school and home can work together. It will also be useful to carry out one or two of the activities in the book with the parents at this time so that they can see the creative and interactive nature of the tasks that their children will be engaging in.
- Each child taking part in the sessions will need a homework book so make sure to involve the parents in this process by jointly agreeing whether school will give each child a book or whether the parents want to buy a

book that their child might choose outside of school. Make sure that this is a collaborative decision between home and school as the homework activities are an integral part of this programme.

- Talk to parents in order to problem-solve with them what will be the best way of letting them know what the homework tasks for the week will be by presenting them with the following examples: writing the homework task objectives directly into the children's homework books, printing them on to labels so that they can stick these into each book easily, or directly sending them in an email home to the parents.
- For each of the 32 activities, you will need to have resources available such as old magazines, food ingredients such as cornflour and food colouring, craft materials, etc. Another way to involve the parents is by putting up a resource list outside of classrooms so that they can volunteer to bring in different items that you might need and that they might have at home. In the same way, parents will need resources for the homework activities so make sure to have some extra available at school, just in case there are parents who might not have what they need at home.
- During the course of carrying out the activities within the programme, you might be covering certain topics such as 'who is in my family', 'strengths', and 'using what I am good at'. It will be useful at these times to invite parents in to school to harness their talents and knowledge such as sharing their own stories of persistence, leading on a craft activity if that is what they do for a living, or as volunteers to support during the sessions (providing that your school have no issues with this with regards to confidentiality, etc.). Being able to match parent's strengths and skills to activities and support needed during the sessions is a great way of involving them in this learning process.
- Think about the children who will be involved in the sessions and their varying needs and family circumstances. Depending on their home situation, there may be times when doing homework might not be the family's top priority. You need to be aware of and acknowledge when this might be the case for some parents and facilitate a solution by asking them, 'what can we do to help?'. If they are not able to do the homework activities with their child, it will be important for a member of school staff to find some time during the school day or week to do the homework tasks with these children so that they do not lose out on opportunities to consolidate their learning.
- Many parents will love the opportunity to be a part of this learning journey but there will be some hard-to-reach parents who do not readily come in to school and do not take an active part in their children's education. Even though this may be the case, it may still be beneficial to offer them a home visit right at the beginning to tell them about the things that their children will be learning at school and the activities that will be involved. Even if they are

not active partners in their child's learning journey, make sure to continue to send information home about what their children are learning and the progress that they are making, as well as examples of all the great things that they have been creating at school. In this way, you are still keeping them informed about what is happening and sharing their children's successes with them, which could over time motivate them to get in touch or become active participants in this process.
- It is important for both children and parents to receive feedback about how the sessions are going, such as regularly sending home information about the children's successes and achievements, which can be as simple as sending parents a 'positive postcard' or 'compliment slips'. At the end of doing all these 32 activities with the children, also make sure to organise a celebration of their work and successes. The children themselves could organise an afternoon party, make their own invitations, and plan out the different ways of showing their parents what they have been doing. They can then end this celebration with some certificates given out by the Head teacher for example, some party snacks, and perhaps even a little bit of dancing.
- It is beneficial to be aware that there might be times when some parents may not respond well to some of the activities, or they might be finding it difficult to manage their children's difficult feelings and behaviour at home. A helpful way to support these parents is to make yourself available to meet with them, and to be flexible in your approach so that you can give them time and space to express their concerns. Make sure to acknowledge and reflect back what they are feeling or finding hard (e.g. 'It sounds from what you are saying that you are worried that . . .'), and be understanding. Doing this will show them that you are not dismissing their concerns or their feelings, but rather that you care and want to understand what they are going through so that together you can find the best way forward.

Working with children with special needs

Given the creative and practical nature of the activities within this programme, it should be able to cater for varying special educational needs with which some children might present. However, this will depend on the individual needs of the children and how much they are able to access in terms of their cognitive ability, their speech and language development, their mobility or medical needs (e.g. visual or hearing impairment), and any specific diagnosis that they might have such as autism or ADHD. Even though the 32 sessions in this programme are visual and practical and allow for movement between activities, some aspects of each session may need to be re-structured or replaced in order to ensure that the children access tasks that are developmentally appropriate. Members of school staff working with children with special needs should thus view this as an adapt-to-need programme that can be changed where needed, in order to make learning as individualised and as relevant as possible for the children taking part.

The first thing to do is to spend some time before the session thinking about the individual needs of the children in the group, and how the activities may therefore need to be adapted. For example, adaptations can be made in situations such as:

- Children who have varying levels of language, or speech and language difficulties, will need access to activities that are more practical in nature and do not rely on the use of language to both understand what they need to do, as well as express their thoughts and ideas.
- Children with physical disabilities or sensory impairments that can affect their access to activities will need resources to be placed close to where they are, as well as being adapted to make them more accessible, such as using more sound-based and highly textured resources for children with a visual impairment.
- You may even need to change some of the activities outlined for some of the sessions if specific issues have arisen for the children during the week (for example: issues at home). An example of a possible scenario is, if a child has just been placed in foster care, it may not be appropriate to work on activities that focus on the topic of 'family'.

Children with special needs will especially benefit from specific activities that enable them to remain focused and engaged in different tasks that aim to support the development of their social and emotional skills, and their learning. When planning for the children with special needs in your group, remember that you are the practitioner who knows them best and who knows what they will respond better to. It will, however, be necessary to consider the following:

- Young children with special needs respond well to sensory activities that involve manipulating everyday items such as moving their hands through rice or pasta, smelling scented objects, and playing with sand and water. Activities that incorporate these practical elements aim to support the children's engagement and exploration, as well as promote calm and relaxation. These kinds of relaxation activities are better suited for children with special needs than tasks that involve listening to guided visualisations, or having to follow specific instructions.
- Allow the children to make choices between a limited number of visual choice cards during the activities as this encourages communication skills, as well as giving the children the opportunity to express their ideas in a way that is more accessible to them. For example, rather than being asked about what makes a good friend, a child with special needs would be better able to distinguish a good from a bad friend if he or

she had pictures about varying friendship qualities in front of them to look at and choose from.
- Make sure that the children are able to access calming and movement breaks away from the noise and busyness of the group during each session. A few minutes in a quiet area will allow a child to calm when the activities become too overwhelming or if they just need a break from being sat down for too long.
- Modify and adapt toys and resources to make them more easily accessible such as using balls and balloons with bells inside (for children with visual difficulties for example), attaching Velcro to pictures and pieces of card for easy assembly (for children with motor difficulties), having pre-made parts of activities that children can use without having to cut and stick things together (for children with attention and learning difficulties), etc.
- Have materials available that the children can use more easily such as using marker pens rather than pencils for ease of recording, and using chubby crayons and brushes with thick handles to make them easier to hold.
- Use visual resources such as a visual timetable for the session, and visual prompt cards to help the children focus on what they need to do.
- Allow the children to work with a peer buddy who can help and prompt them during an activity.
- Using digital technology such as accessing songs and stories as video clips on an electronic whiteboard will be beneficial, as well as using tablets to support the children to communicate their ideas and choices.
- Where possible, use real-life examples of objects that you are displaying as pictures during activities, such as having a ball and a skipping rope alongside their corresponding pictures if these are things that the children like playing with when they are with their friends.
- Make sure that all resources and materials are accessible to the children such as placing items in containers with short sides to make them easier to reach, attaching pens and toys to tables so that they do not roll out of reach or fall, and removing obstacles near the children to allow them to move around freely.

Section 3 – Relationships

Human beings are born as social individuals and as such have the ability to build and maintain positive relationships that are essential to our mental health, our emotional wellbeing, and to the way we behave in our society. A relationship is a bond created by developing a close connection with someone else. It is that feeling of being connected to family and friends, to groups, or to a community. This includes our parents, siblings, friends, teachers, neighbours, and many other people who help us and are part of our lives. From a young age, the relationships that children build and maintain with others within their environment and daily lives shape the way that they see the world and affect all areas of their development.

The early emotional bonds that babies and young children build between themselves and their parents or carers are called attachments, which are developed from positive and appropriate reciprocal communication and interactions. These initial attachments are fundamental to a child's overall progress as they influence their emotional, social, and cognitive development from being an infant, into their primary years, and then further into the future.

When a secure bond or attachment is established between a child and their parent, the child begins to develop appropriate social skills, the ability to understand and express emotions, and to adapt and problem-solve when faced with negative emotions or difficult situations. They develop their self-awareness, their feelings of confidence and self-worth, and their ability to cooperate, work, and empathise with others. This not only impacts on a child's ability to develop friendships with others in the early and primary years, but continues to influence the success of all other future relationships in both their teenage years and further into adulthood.

In order to build secure attachments, babies and young children need parents and caregivers to respond to their needs and expressions in a positive way, and by providing them with comfort, attention, love, and security. If this does not occur, then children begin to grow with a sense that their needs will not be met, that no-one will help and comfort them, and that ultimately they are unloved and unsafe. This leads to the development of insecure or disorganised attachments with associated difficulties related to an inability to self-regulate and to build positive relationships, and to avoid and at times sabotage proximity and care offered by others around them. This further leads to the presentation of difficult behaviour due to feelings of distress, anger, and a lack of capacity to cope with tricky situations. Children with these types of difficult attachments therefore need encouragement, support, and opportunities to develop the skills needed to build successful relationships and to foster positive mental health.

The development of close, trusting, and loving relationships early on sets the foundation for the success of all future relationships. Enabling children to grow and flourish in the context of close relationships will provide them with love, nurturing, trust, and understanding. These factors will not only support children to build dependable and meaningful relationships with others, but will also aim to reduce difficulties associated with loneliness, isolation, and challenging behaviour.

A vital part of a young child's life is therefore to be able to develop positive relationships with their parents and other influential adults such as their teachers, as well as build and maintain friendships with peers. In order to do this, they need to access an environment that enables them to flourish and opportunities to develop early skills that will ensure that they thrive both emotionally and socially. During the early years of child development, children need to learn about recognising the qualities and traits of a good friend, as well as begin building the skills needed to foster friendships with others, which includes knowing how to treat others and be kind. As part of this learning process, it is necessary for supportive adults to both model and spend time working with children to help them to develop these skills, which is one of the main aims of this programme. This joint working and interaction, both at school and at home, will ensure that children are exposed to positive relationships and supported to focus on building their own so that as they grow and progress, they are then able to independently connect with others in their own lives.

The activities within this programme that aim to support the development of relationships therefore focus on recognising what a good friend is and how each of us have positive friendship qualities to offer each other, as well as knowing who makes up our family and friendship circles. This then extends to beginning to think about how to make and sustain friendships with others, as well as being able to reflect on what we like doing with our friends and how we can show kindness towards those around us.

14   Relationships

Session 1

Learning objective

- I know what a good friend is

Settling-down poem

Before the children sit down in their group, the first thing to do is to introduce them to the settling-down poem, and tell them that they will be able to hear and practise this poem every time they come together in this group. This poem will help them to know when it is time to start the session. It may be helpful to have this poem written down on a large piece of card, with sentences used alongside pictures as prompts for the children to learn the words and actions.

> '**Here are my ears, I can hear** *(with the action of touching their ears)*
> **Here are my eyes, I can see** *(with the action of touching their eyes)*
> **Here is my heart, I can feel** *(with the action of holding their hands to their heart)*
> **Here is my friend, next to me** *(with the action of holding hands with friends next to them)*
> **I am ready to learn and play** *(with the action of swinging their hands together)*
> **I'm sitting down, legs crossed, hooray!**' *(with the action of sitting with their legs crossed)*

Introduction to the group

You will initially need to introduce the children to this programme by talking to them about how they are going to work together in this group every week, which will give them the opportunity to engage in different activities and learn new skills. In order to build their sense of belonging and exclusivity within this group, ask the children what they would like to call the group, which will be a special name that only those children in the group will know (e.g. Super Stars or Clever Cats). Then, using a big piece of sugar paper or card, help the children to brainstorm some clear rules for the group (three or four maximum), and introduce them to the reward system that you have chosen to use during the sessions.

Warm-up game

Ask the children to sit in a circle so that you can play the 'Swap Places' game together. The aim of this game is for the children to swap places with each other when you give out a phrase that includes something that they have in common such as their eye or hair colour. As the game progresses, make sure to increase the complexity of these phrases to prompt the children to listen carefully and to identify others with a range of similar skills and attributes. Some examples of the phrases that you could offer could be as follows:

- Swap places if you have brown eyes.
- Swap places if you have a dog.
- Swap places if you live in a house.
- Swap places if you like to sing and dance.
- Swap places if you can swim and ride a bicycle.
- Swap places if you speak English and another language.
- Swap places if you have a brother and a sister and a dog.
- Swap places if you like pizza and ice-cream and cake.
- Swap places if you have been on a train but not a plane.
- Swap places if you like to swim in the pool but not in the sea.

Main activity

Read a few short stories to the children that have positive friendships as their main focus, in order to try and identify with them what each story highlights as the main qualities of a friend. As you read a story and look through the book together, encourage the children to look at the qualities that the characters may be demonstrating in terms of what they do for each other and what they say that is positive. Once you have identified these traits with the children, record each of them on separate big pieces of paper as basic drawings and words. Then, lay out lots of coloured markers, crayons, and art and craft materials, and let the children decorate each piece of paper in colourful and varied ways. Some examples of picture books that may be relevant for this activity are:

- *Toot and Puddle: You Are My Sunshine* by Holly Hobbie
- *Friends* by Helme Heine

16 Relationships

- *Those Shoes* by Maribeth Boelts and Noah Jones
- *You Are Friendly* by Todd Snow and Melodee Strong
- *How to Be a Friend: A Guide to Making Friends and Keeping Them* by Laurene Brown

Relaxation

The day before the session, you will need to prepare some coloured and scented dry rice for the children to use. You will need some rice, food colouring of several colours, and a couple of different essential oils (e.g. lavender, jasmine, and peppermint). Divide your dry rice into a few plastic bags and in each bag, add a few drops of different types of food colouring. Close and shake the bag so that you mix the colour with all the rice, and when this is done, add a few drops of a different essential oil to each bag. Close and shake the bags again so that the fragrance spreads throughout all of the rice. When this is done, lay out the rice on different trays and leave over night to dry. You will therefore have a few types of dry rice for the session, with different colours and scents. You can leave this rice in their individual trays or lay it out on large plastic sheets on the floor. The children can then spend some time quietly playing with the rice by touching it, moving it around, allowing it to escape through their fingers, and taking in their varied scents, whilst listening to calm and relaxing music.

Resources

- Settling-down poem on a large piece of card and music (if needed)
- Stories and picture books about friendship
- Large pieces of sugar paper or card
- Coloured pens or markers, and crayons
- Art and craft materials such as glue, tissue paper, sequins, gems, pipe cleaners, etc.
- Dry rice, plastic zip-lock bags, trays, and large plastic sheets (if needed)
- Different types of food colouring and essential oils
- Relaxing music
- Homework books

Homework

With the help of an adult, the children need to gather up and look through a few of their story books at home to try and find examples of when they can spot the characters being good friends to each other. They can then choose one or a few of these examples and draw pictures of them in their homework books, which the supporting adult can then help them to label or caption.

Session 2

Learning objective

- I know that I am a good friend.

Settling-down poem

'Here are my ears, I can hear,
Here are my eyes, I can see,
Here is my heart, I can feel,
Here is my friend, next to me,
I am ready to learn and play,
I'm sitting down, legs crossed, hooray!'

Warm-up game

Before the start of the session, fill a soft material bag with lots of different objects and toys of different sizes, shapes, and textures. The children then have to close their eyes and reach inside the bag for an object; once they have chosen an object they then have to try and describe it to the group without pulling it out of the bag. Once the group has made a few attempts at trying to guess what the object might be, the child can then pull it out and show everyone. The group can then clap if they managed to figure out what the object is correctly and then the next child has a go at choosing an object; do this until everyone has had a turn at choosing a toy from the bag.

Main activity

Take out the large pieces of paper from the previous session that show different characteristics and qualities of a good friend, and remind the children what these were. Once you have done this, give each child a different coloured happy-face sticker and ask them to move around and place a sticker on each of the pieces of paper that represent what they feel makes them a good friend. For example, if a child feels that he or she is a good friend because they help others and are kind, then they would place a happy-face sticker on the sheet of paper where you have created a drawing for being kind, and then on the other piece of paper where you have created a drawing for being helpful. Once all the children have had an opportunity to do this, you can then look at the pieces of paper as a group and check how each child is similar or different to each other in terms of what they feel makes them a good friend.

Relaxation

Have silver or gold card available for the children to use, as well as strips of red, orange, and yellow paper (e.g. tissue paper). Using a stapler or some sticky tape, help each child roll and stick a piece of silver or gold card to create a cylinder. Then, the children stick strips of the orange, red, and yellow paper to one end of their cylinder. Once this is done, they can then use this to help them with a breathing exercise. They place the open end of the cylinder over their mouths and then practise breathing in and out slowly, and as they do so, they can watch the strips of paper moving inwards and outwards. This enables them to visually see how their breathing is working and allows them to control how they are breathing by what they see the strips of paper doing.

Resources

- Settling-down poem and music (if needed)
- Soft material bag with varied objects and toys
- Large pieces of paper from the previous session
- Happy-face stickers of different colours
- Silver and gold card
- Strips of yellow, orange, and red paper (e.g. tissue paper) or ribbon
- Stapler, sticky tape, and scissors
- Homework books

Homework

The children need to look back at the pictures that they have drawn in their homework books of characters that they had found in stories showing qualities of good friends. They can then draw a smiley face or a tick next to each drawing if they feel that they are also a good friend in the same way as is depicted in the drawing. If they remember other qualities that make them a good friend that they have not yet drawn, they can draw these in their books too.

Session 3

Learning objective

- I know who my friends are and why

Settling-down poem

> *'Here are my ears, I can hear,*
> *Here are my eyes, I can see,*
> *Here is my heart, I can feel,*
> *Here is my friend, next to me,*
> *I am ready to learn and play,*
> *I'm sitting down, legs crossed, hooray!'*

Warm-up game

Have a bag filled with lots of different objects and then ask the first child to take out an object and complete the sentence 'I went to the shop and bought a …'. Once the first child has done this, pass the bag to the next child who takes out another object and says 'I went to the shop and bought a … and a …' so as to include the object taken out by the first child. As you move along the group, the sentence will get longer and the children will have to try hard to remember what the others have picked out of the bag before them. Play this for two or three rounds, depending on time, and start each round with different children and different objects. Encourage the children to help each other out if they are finding it hard to remember all the objects in the right order.

Main activity

Make sure to have the large pieces of paper from the previous sessions available, which outline the qualities of a good friend. Place these on the floor so that the children can reach them and then remind them of each of the characteristics that you have drawn on each individual sheet. Next, give each child a handful of small pieces of paper and a pen or pencil, and ask them to draw each of their friends on separate pieces of paper (encourage them to draw friends from both in and outside of school). When they have done this, they then have to look at the different qualities on the big sheets of paper and place each picture that they have drawn of their friends on the large piece of paper that they think is the best friendly characteristic of each of their friends. For example, if they have drawn a picture of their friend Tom and feel that his best friendly quality is being helpful, then they place their drawing of Tom on the large sheet of paper that corresponds with 'being helpful'. At the end of the activity, the children can then take the pictures that they have drawn of their friends and stick them into their homework books, and colour them in. If you have time, go round and write down the quality for each of the children's friends underneath the pictures that they have glued into their books.

Relaxation

Get a tennis ball or a hard squeezy ball for each child to use. Ask each child to place a ball in their right hand and pretend it is an orange that they need to squeeze to get all of the juice out. Encourage them to squeeze their ball as hard as they can with just one hand and imagine squeezing all the juice out. Ask them to focus on the tightness that they can feel in their hand and their arm as they squeeze. After squeezing the ball a few times with their right hand, ask them to move the ball over to their left hand and carry out the same squeezing activity. When they have done this a few times with their left hand, they can drop the ball on the floor, shake out their hands and arms, and focus on how relaxed their hands and arms now feel.

Resources

- Settling-down poem and music (if needed)
- Bag filled with small objects and toys
- Large pieces of paper from the last session with friendship qualities
- Small pieces of paper
- Pens, pencils, and colouring pencils, markers, or crayons
- Glue sticks

20   Relationships

- Tennis balls or hard squeezy balls
- Homework books

Homework

If the children were not able to finish colouring in the pictures that they have drawn of their friends, they can do this for homework. They can talk to their parents about each friend and what they feel is each friend's best friendship quality. From this, they can then start thinking about other people around them (such as their family and teachers) and think about whether they can notice these friendly characteristics in them as well. If so, the children can draw pictures of those around them, and their parents can note down what friendly quality the child has chosen to describe each of them.

Session 4

Learning objective

- I know who is in my family

Settling-down poem

> 'Here are my ears, I can hear,
> Here are my eyes, I can see,
> Here is my heart, I can feel,
> Here is my friend, next to me,
> I am ready to learn and play,
> I'm sitting down, legs crossed, hooray!'

Warm-up game

Find a simple line drawing that the children will need to colour in and make one copy for each child in the group. Give each child their own copy as well as a few colouring pencils that they can use to colour in different parts of their drawing when you offer them a statement that might be relevant to them. For example, if it is a picture of a teddy bear, you can give them a statement such as 'If you have a brother, colour the teddy's eyes in blue. If you have a sister, colour the teddy's eyes in brown'. You can choose whatever statements you want to use as a way of getting the children to answer questions about themselves in a creative way. At the end, the children can share their pictures with the group so that all can see how they are similar or different. Some example statements could be:

- If you have a dog, colour one of teddy's arms in yellow.
- If you can roll your tongue, colour teddy's tummy in orange.
- If you have a special friend, colour teddy's heart in red.
- If you have a big family, colour teddy's right leg in green.

- If you can ride a bicycle, colour teddy's left ear in brown.
- If you can hop on one leg, colour teddy's left leg in blue.

Main activity

Before the start of the session, go through a variety of old newspapers and magazines, or browse images on the internet and find pictures of different people of varying ages. Cut these out or print them out so that you can use them with the children. Show the children each picture in turn and ask them what age they think the person in the picture might be, and given what they see, whether they think that the person in each picture could be someone's brother, or mother, or grandfather, or aunt, or cousin, among others. As you and the children classify each picture into different categories that can include brother, sister, Mum, Dad, Grandma, Grandpa, aunt, uncle, etc., place these in separate piles on the floor. Then, give each child a plastic hoop and ask them to choose pictures from each pile to go into their hoops that show different people that they know are in their family. At the end of the activity, you can then look at each other's hoops and ask the children if they can tell you about the pictures that they have chosen and how they link to who is in their family.

Relaxation

Give each child a teddy or large-ish soft toy that they can easily cuddle. Get them to lie on their backs on the floor and to follow your instructions as you tell them to breathe in to the count of 1,2,3,4,5 whilst they hug their teddy tight, and then release the cuddle as they breathe out to the count of 1,2,3,4,5. Continue doing this a few times and encouraging the children to focus on their breathing, whilst relaxing music is playing in the background.

Resources

- Settling-down poem and music (if needed)
- Copies of colouring pages for each child and colouring pencils
- Pictures from magazines, newspapers, or the internet
- A plastic hoop for each child
- Glue sticks
- Large teddies and soft toys
- Relaxing music
- Homework books

Homework

Let the children stick the family pictures that they chose to go into their plastic hoops during the main activity, into their homework books. If you have time, you can then label these pictures for them or they can have a go at writing the words down themselves. Their homework is to then collect photographs of their family and stick these into their books, and with support if needed, label who everyone is.

22 Relationships

Session 5

Learning objective

- I know how to make friends

Settling-down poem

> 'Here are my ears, I can hear,
> Here are my eyes, I can see,
> Here is my heart, I can feel,
> Here is my friend, next to me,
> I am ready to learn and play,
> I'm sitting down, legs crossed, hooray!'

Warm-up game

Play the 'I sent a letter to . . . ' game with the children by asking them to close their eyes and you can then choose one child to take a letter around the outside of the circle. The child taking it round then quietly places the letter in the lap of another child that they choose. The chosen child then has to hide it quickly and pretend that they do not have it. Once this has been done, ask the rest of the group to open their eyes and they then have to try and guess who has the letter. When someone guesses correctly, then they have a turn at taking the letter round the circle to choose someone to give it to, and so on. Let every child have a few chances at playing this game and when you have finished, open the letter and share around something that you have placed inside (e.g. funny pictures, stickers, etc.).

Main activity

Using the large pieces of paper with the friendship qualities from the previous sessions, recap with the children what kinds of characteristics and behaviours they notice about themselves and their friends that make them good friends to have. You can then begin to link this to specific kinds of things that they can do that will help them make friends. For example: for the 'kindness' quality, something that will help them make friends is by being kind to others, which might include sharing some of your lunch with another child if they do not have any of their own. Or for the 'being helpful' quality, what could help them make friends could be helping someone when they are finding something tricky. The purpose of this activity is to therefore support the children to think about ways that they can make friends by using the friendship qualities as prompts for some ideas. As you and the children come up with specific ideas to help them make friends, record these as drawings and words on an extra-large piece of card, in order to create a big 'This is how we make friends' poster. When you have collected lots of ideas on your card, ask the children to help you draw, colour in, and decorate the poster so that they can fully participate in creating this together. This poster can then be displayed somewhere central in school where all of the children can see it.

Relaxation

This activity will help the children relax their muscles by following a set of instructions, whilst you model what they have to do. They have to sit on a chair and follow these steps:

- Make the biggest happy face you can with a huge smile, and hold it for five seconds: 5, 4, 3, 2, 1, and relax.
- Make the angriest face you can; really wrinkle up your eyes and lips, and hold it for five seconds: 5, 4, 3, 2, 1, and relax.
- Stretch your arms out in front of you as much as you can, pretend you're pushing a wall as hard as you can and hold it for five seconds: 5, 4, 3, 2, 1, and relax.
- Stretch your arms out to your sides as much as you can and close your hands into a fist. Hold them closed as tight as possible for five seconds: 5, 4, 3, 2, 1, and relax.

24   Relationships

- Hold onto your chair with your hands and push your back against your chair as hard as you can, and hold for five seconds: 5, 4, 3, 2, 1, and relax.
- Push out your tummy, make it as hard as you can, and hold for five seconds: 5, 4, 3, 2, 1, and relax.
- Press your legs together really tight and hold for five seconds: 5, 4, 3, 2, 1, and relax.
- Hold onto your chair with your hands and bend your knees up to your tummy, and hold for five seconds: 5, 4, 3, 2, 1, and relax.
- Stretch your legs out in front of you as high as they can go and hold for five seconds: 5, 4, 3, 2, 1, and relax.
- Curl your toes in as much as you can and hold for five seconds: 5, 4, 3, 2, 1, and relax.

Resources

- Settling-down poem and music (if needed)
- Letter with treats inside (e.g. stickers, labels, pictures, etc.)
- Large pieces of paper from the previous sessions with friendship qualities
- Extra-large piece of card, pens, pencils, and coloured markers
- Art and craft materials for decoration
- Photographs of the poster created (if there is a digital camera available in school)
- Homework books

Homework

If possible, it would be useful to take a photograph of the poster that you and the children have created during the session, and then make several copies that you can stick into each of the children's homework books. The children can then show this to their parents and can therefore use this photograph as an example of a friendship poster that each child can create at home. They can take their time to make their very own posters with their parents, siblings and friends at home, and then if possible, take a photograph of what they have created and also stick this into their homework books to share with others at school.

Session 6

Learning objective

- I know how to keep my friends

Settling-down poem

'Here are my ears, I can hear,
Here are my eyes, I can see,
Here is my heart, I can feel,
Here is my friend, next to me,

*I am ready to learn and play,
I'm sitting down, legs crossed, hooray!'*

Warm-up game

Before the session starts, get a picture of each of the main body parts, such as the head, ears, eyes, nose, mouth, neck, arms, fingers, toes, legs, tummy, etc. Fold these pictures and when the children are settled, ask each of them to pick one. They can then open their pictures up to see the one that they got, but rather than showing it to the rest of the group, they have to describe what it is. The group then has to try and identify what body part it is. Once all the body parts are identified, give each child a big piece of paper and they have to draw a big picture of the body part that they got. When they have done this, help them to cut out their body parts and then stick each of them together in the correct order to make up a large, and funny, body!

Main activity

Give each child a piece of card and they can help each other to draw around each other's hands with colourful markers or crayons. Make sure that the children draw around both hands and they can then cut them out. Collect everyone's hands and then using sticky tape, glue, or staples, stick them together to create a long paper chain of hands. Then tell the children that you are going to work out what they can do to keep their friends by thinking of two different choices. Give them two choices of things that they can do, and they have to decide which one they need to do to keep their friends, rather than lose them. For example, some of their choices could be:

Positive choice	*Negative choice*
Talk to your friends	Ignore your friends
Play with your friends	Play by yourself
Share your toys	Don't share your toys
Help your friends	Don't help your friends
Listen to your friends	Don't listen to your friends
Be kind to your friends	Be mean to your friends
If you're angry, talk to your friends	If you're angry, hit your friends

Once you have come up with as many positive choices as you can, you can then record each of these, as drawings or words, on each of the hands that make up the hand chain that you have created. If you have time, the children can then decorate the chain with pens, pencils, or arts and craft materials. This then becomes your 'Friendship Hands' chain that can be hung up in the room as a reminder of the things that they can do to help them with their friendships.

Relaxation

Have play dough of different colours available for the children to use, as well as a small zip-lock bag for every child. Ask the children to take a piece of play-dough from every different colour and place it inside their bag, and then help them to zip up their bag by keeping as little air inside it as possible. Once their bags are closed up nice and tight, put some relaxing music on and the children can spend some time squashing, rolling, and squeezing their playdough, and watching as all the colours start mixing together to create a rainbow of different colours.

Resources

- Settling-down poem and music (if needed)
- Pictures of body parts
- A big piece of paper for every child
- Marker pens, pencils, and crayons
- Pieces of card
- Scissors, sticky tape, glue, or staples
- Arts and craft materials
- Play dough of different colours and a zip-lock bag for every child
- Relaxing music
- Homework books

Homework

The children need to draw around their hands several times in their homework books and then take it round to their siblings, parents, and other family members, to ask them what they do to keep their friends. With help, each of these things can then be recorded on each of the hands that they have drawn, either as drawings or words. They could even ask their friends or adults at school so that they can collect lots of ideas of things that can be done to keep friends.

Session 7

Learning objective

- I know what I like doing with my friends

Settling-down poem

> 'Here are my ears, I can hear,
> Here are my eyes, I can see,

Here is my heart, I can feel,
Here is my friend, next to me,
I am ready to learn and play,
I'm sitting down, legs crossed, hooray!'

Warm-up game

Have one balloon for every child in the group, each of a different colour, and inflate these before the start of the session. The fun starts when you give each child their own balloon, which they throw up into the air and then have to stop from touching the floor. They need to keep their eye on their own balloon and follow it round, hitting it so that it stays in the air, no matter where they have to move and how. The winner is the child who can keep their balloon in their air for the longest time.

Main activity

Get four pieces of card of different colours and stick each one in each of the four corners of the room. The children start off by standing in the centre of the room but then need to move around according to what they like doing with their friends, given the prompts that you offer them. Examples of some prompts that you could use are:

- If you like running around with your friends, go to the green corner.
- If you like playing in the park with your friends, go to the red corner.
- If you like eating ice-cream with your friends, go to the yellow corner.
- If you like drawing with your friends, go to the blue corner.
- If you like singing with your friends, go to the green corner.
- If you like playing video games with your friends, go to the red corner.
- If you like playing hide-and-seek with your friends, go to the yellow corner.
- If you like dancing with your friends, go to the blue corner.

Before the session, make a list of the prompts that you are going to offer the children and then collect small pictures depicting these different scenarios (e.g. a picture of children playing in the park), which you can then photocopy so that these are available for the children at the end of the activity so that they can stick them in their homework books.

The aim of the activity is for you to offer the children a prompt, and whoever likes doing that activity with their friends, moves to the corresponding colour. As they do this, on a large piece of paper, you can tally up how many children like doing certain things so that at the end, you can look for differences and similarities in the things that the children like doing with their friends. You can then lay out the pictures of the prompt scenarios that you gathered earlier and ask the children to choose pictures of the things that they said they like doing with their friends, which they can then stick into their homework books.

Relaxation

Have a plastic see-through container for each child (e.g. a plastic jar or bottle), with lids to shut them tight. The children need to fill their containers up with water and then add to it a few drops of whatever colour of food colouring that they want. Next, they add a spoonful of glitter and some gems or sequins to their water, and with help, close their containers so that they are closed as tightly as possible. Put on some relaxing music and the children have to listen to the music as they play with their newly created sensory jars, watching the glitter and gems swirling around as they gently shake and roll the container.

Resources

- Settling-down poem and music (if needed)
- A balloon of every colour, one for each child
- Four pieces of different coloured card, a large piece of paper, and pens
- Copies of small pictures of prompt scenarios, and glue sticks
- A plastic jar or bottle for each child (with lids)
- Water, different colours of food colouring, glitter, gems, and sequins
- Relaxing music
- Homework books

Homework

As part of the main activity, the children stuck pictures in their books of things that they like doing with their friends. For homework, they have to find more pictures (e.g. cut out from old magazines) that they can stick into their homework books, or do some drawings of other things that they also like doing with their friends.

Session 8

Learning objective

- I know how to do something kind for others

Settling-down poem

> 'Here are my ears, I can hear,
> Here are my eyes, I can see,
> Here is my heart, I can feel,
> Here is my friend, next to me,
> I am ready to learn and play,
> I'm sitting down, legs crossed, hooray!'

Warm-up game

Ask the children to move around the room in order to find as many small objects or toys as they can, and then bring them to you. Once you have collected a big pile of items, you and the children can look at them and decide on lots of different ways that you could sort them (e.g. sort them by colour, size, or function). Using plastic hoops that have been placed around the room, once you have decided on one way of sorting the items, the children can start sorting them into different hoops. When you have sorted all the items into hoops according to one category (e.g. colour), you can then start all over again by sorting them into a different category.

Main activity

Have a variety of old magazines available for the children to look through and from which to cut out relevant pictures, as well as some pictures that you have collected before the start of the session (for backup). On a big piece of paper, draw a huge red heart and explain to the children that they are going to find pictures of people being kind to each other, as well as pictures of things that you can do or give to someone when you are being kind (e.g. a flower). Once you have collected a variety of different pictures, you can start placing them inside the heart that you have drawn to create a 'Kindness Heart'. When there are lots of pictures inside the heart, ask the children to pick one picture of something kind that they would like to do for someone else, tell everyone who they would like to do it for, and then stick this picture down in their homework books. When they have done this, you can then stick down all the remaining pictures in the heart so that you can keep it as a visual reminder of lots of kind things that you can do for others.

Relaxation

Before the session, find a simple set of colouring patterns and enlarge them so that each child has got a big page to use (e.g. A3 size). Tell the children that they are going to spend some time colouring in their patterns whilst listening to relaxing music, which means it has to be 'quiet time' when they are not talking to each other. Put on some calm music and let the colouring begin!

Resources

- Settling-down poem and music (if needed)
- Hoops
- Large piece of paper and red marker pen
- Magazines and pictures from the internet focusing on kind acts
- Scissors and glue sticks
- Colouring patterns from books or the internet, enlarged to A3 size
- Relaxing music
- Homework books

Relationships

Homework

The children will have stuck into their homework books a picture of something kind that they would like to do for someone else. Their homework is to look through old magazines or newspapers at home to find more kindness pictures, cut these out, and then stick them in their books. With support, they can then label who they will be doing these acts of kindness for, and they can then start doing these acts for the people that they have chosen.

Section 4 – Emotions

Babies are born with the ability to feel and express basic emotions related to feeling hungry or frustrated, experiencing pain or discomfort, and feeling happy by smiling or upset by crying. Children continue learning about emotions from a very young age depending on the environment in which they find themselves, as well as the relationships that they have built with their parents and caregivers. The building blocks for successful emotional development depends on these early relationships; the care and nurturing that they receive from those around them has a substantial impact on their understanding and expression of emotions. The importance of building strong bonds with their parents and carers enables children to access love, comfort, and the help that they need to deal with a range of emotions, which in turn supports their ability to communicate their own needs, as well as understand the needs of others. This encourages the development of vital skills needed to recognise their own and the feelings of others, express their emotions in a socially appropriate way, deal with negative emotions when faced with tricky situations, and to be able to calm when they feel that they are not coping.

Children will experience a range of emotions on a daily basis but their ability to respond to these will have an impact on their development, their behaviour, and their ability to deal with varying situations. Emotional development begins in early childhood when babies begin to display emotions such as joy, sadness, fear, anger, and surprise. Through increased self-awareness and experience of the world, and the development of their emotional intelligence as they get older, children are then able to demonstrate more complex emotions such as worry, embarrassment, excitement, guilt, pride, and empathy. As these emotions emerge, they need to start identifying them in order to develop their understanding of why they occur in themselves and in others, as well as begin to develop the skills to manage them when they are faced with difficult situations.

As children grow up, the way that they feel is increasingly influenced by their thoughts and the way that others react to these feelings. If those around them acknowledge and validate their emotions, this allows them to begin to structure their thinking in terms of developing the ability to recognise what they are feeling and reflect on what others are feeling too. The ability to recognise and manage emotions in this way is an important skill needed for self-regulation, but sometimes children can find this difficult to do. There are a number of elements that can influence how well children can understand and express their emotions such as each child's individual personality, how their needs have been met by others, and the beliefs that they have adopted from those around them about how to communicate what they are feeling. Other factors such as stress, illness, violence or trauma, difficult circumstances within families, and learning difficulties, will also impact on how able children are to appropriately express and manage their emotions. At times, this can result in children displaying difficult feelings such as anger, frustration, and fear in inappropriate ways, which affects their wellbeing, development, communication, friendships, learning, and their social behaviour. It is therefore vital that adults support and teach children from a young age to recognise, understand, and deal with their emotions in an appropriate way. This needs to include developing the skills needed to problem-solve ways of coping with emotional challenges and continue to apply these to their daily lives.

Emotional regulation is the ability to control our emotions by monitoring and recognising a variety of different feelings, as well as adapting how we feel in a way that is appropriate to a given situation. This does not mean ignoring or trying to reduce negative emotions but knowing how to express them fully in a way that benefits us socially and emotionally. Regulating our emotions is an integral part of developing emotional intelligence as this includes the ability to understand how our feelings and thoughts are connected, using this understanding to problem-solve solutions to emotional obstacles, whilst also being able to reflect on how others express, manage, and are influenced by how we feel.

Emotional intelligence has a positive impact on children's ability to learn, their level of empathy, their engagement in prosocial behaviour, their self-expression, and their adaptability in various contexts and situations that involve negative emotions. Being aware of their emotions and being able to self-regulate will therefore affect their school learning, their engagement and success, their ability to cope in their daily lives, and to build strong relationships with others.

The activities within this programme that aim to support the development of emotional awareness therefore focus on young children recognising when they and others feel happy and sad, as well as reflecting on what situations and circumstances lead to them feeling this way. The activities within this section also include recognising anger and being able to reflect on what may cause the children to feel this way, which also needs to incorporate opportunities for them to begin to think of ways to make both themselves and others feel better when they are dealing with negative emotions.

Session 1

Learning objective

- I know when I feel happy or sad

Settling-down poem

'Here are my ears, I can hear,
Here are my eyes, I can see,
Here is my heart, I can feel,
Here is my friend, next to me,
I am ready to learn and play,
I'm sitting down, legs crossed, hooray!'

Warm-up game

Using masking tape, stick two lines of tape on the floor and make sure that they are about one metre apart. On one line write the word 'Start' and on the second line write the word 'Finish'. Give each child a small pom-pom ball and a straw, and then encourage them to have a race in pairs by moving their pom-pom from the start to the finish line by only blowing through their straw. The first child to cross the finish line gives the rest of the group a funny action to do (e.g. hop on one leg whilst holding your nose), and when the group have finished doing this action, then two more children can have a go at racing each other until everyone has had a turn.

Main activity

Before the start of the session, collect a few picture books about feeling happy and sad. Below are a few examples of some helpful books:

- *When I'm Feeling Happy* by Trace Moroney
- *Everybody Feels Happy* by Moira Butterfield
- *If You're Happy and You Know It* by Jan Ormerod
- *When I'm Feeling Sad* by Trace Moroney
- *Everybody Feels Sad* by Moira Butterfield
- *When I Feel Sad* by Cornelia Maude Spelman

Read a few of the happy stories to the children and ask them what the characters are doing that show that they are feeling happy, such as smiling, singing, and jumping. Once you and the children spot these things, write each of these down as words on individual pieces of yellow card. Once you have done this, move on to reading a few of the sad stories to the children, and ask them what the characters are doing that show that they are feeling sad, such as crying, walking with their head down, or sitting curled up on the floor. When you and the children spot these different things, write each one down as words on individual pieces of blue card.

The second part of the activity is to let each child choose one of the yellow pieces of card and one of the blue pieces, and they then need to draw a picture of the words on their cards in order to pictorially show what each word means. At the end of this activity, lay out all of the yellow and blue pieces of card and ask the children which ones they do when they are feeling happy and sad, and for each that they choose, give them yellow and blue pom-poms or counters that they can keep.

Relaxation

Make sure that you have one teddy bear per child available; once each child has chosen the one that they want, ask them to lie on their backs on the floor and to place the teddy on their belly. Help the children to practise deep breathing by breathing in through their nose, pretending that they are smelling a lovely flower, and then slowly breathing out through their mouth, pretending that they are blowing out a candle. Repeat this process several times and encourage the children to watch the movement that the teddy makes on their belly as they breathe in and out. Have some relaxing music playing in the background to help the children feel calm.

Resources

- Settling-down poem and music (if needed)
- Masking tape
- Coloured pom-poms
- Straws
- Picture books about feeling happy and sad
- Pieces of yellow and blue card
- Marker pens and pencils
- Yellow pom-poms or counters
- Blue pom-poms or counters
- A teddy for each child
- Relaxing music
- Homework books

Homework

The children take their yellow and blue pom-poms or counters home, and then stick these down in their homework books. With support from an adult, they then draw pictures and write words for each of them to show what they represent in terms of what they do when they are feeling happy and sad. Yellow pom-poms or counters should represent how the children act when they are feeling happy, and the blue pom-poms or counters should represent how the children act when they are feeling sad.

Session 2

Learning objective

- I know when others feel happy or sad

Settling-down poem

> 'Here are my ears, I can hear,
> Here are my eyes, I can see,
> Here is my heart, I can feel,
> Here is my friend, next to me,
> I am ready to learn and play,
> I'm sitting down, legs crossed, hooray! '

36 Emotions

Warm-up game

Play the 'Pass the Puppet' game where the children sit in a circle and pass a puppet round, whilst you try and make the group laugh. The first child to laugh as the puppet is going round the circle then has to hold the puppet and say as many of something as they can remember (e.g. as many animals, colours, sweets, etc. as possible), once you have told them what they need to name. Once they run out of things to say, they win a prize such as a sticker, and the puppet then moves round the circle until the next person laughs and has to name something different. Play this game so that everyone has a chance to name something and to win a prize.

Main activity

Have the pieces of yellow and blue cards from the previous session available, which highlight different ways of how you can show that you are happy and sad. Lay these out on the floor and let the children look at them to recap on what they found and what they drew about when describing how they act when they are feeling happy or sad. Get two different containers and fill one with yellow counters and one with blue ones, and then take the children out on a search, whilst also taking the yellow and blue pieces of card with you. Walk around the school with the children and ask them to look at the people that they can see around them. If they spot someone who is feeling happy, they are given a yellow counter to hold, and if they spot someone who is feeling sad, they are given a blue counter. If there are not enough people around the school at the time, take the children to the library and ask them to look through picture books and try and find pictures of people or characters feeling happy and sad, and then collecting counters for each that they find. Then, place the yellow and blue pieces of card on the floor and ask the children to place their counters on what they found and observed in others, and then count each one up to see which has been spotted more times and is the most common behaviour seen when someone is feeling happy or sad.

Relaxation

In order to continue practising deep breathing, it is useful to have a variety of materials that will help the children to learn to breathe in and out deeply. Examples of some of these will be resources such as:

- Strongly scented flowers for breathing in.
- Scented perfumes and creams for breathing in.
- Lit candles for blowing out.
- Balloons for blowing up.
- Straws for blowing through.

Have a variety of materials, such as the ones listed here, available for the children to focus and practise their deep breathing with some prompting from you, and whilst listening to relaxing music. You can encourage the children to try using some of these materials whilst they are standing up, then sitting down, and then lying down, to see which way they find helps them to feel the most calm.

Resources

- Settling-down poem and music (if needed)
- Puppet
- Prizes such as stickers
- Yellow and blue pieces of card from the previous session
- Two containers
- Yellow and blue counters
- Materials for deep breathing (e.g. flowers, perfume, creams, candles, balloons, straws, etc.)
- Relaxing music
- Homework books

Homework

Since the last homework session was for the children to draw pictures and with support write words to represent the yellow and blue pom-poms showing happy and sad behaviours, this session's homework is for them to try and observe these behaviours in others around them. They can then place a tick or mark of their choosing next to each pom-pom, depending on what happy and sad behaviours they notice in their families, friends, and out in their community.

Session 3

Learning objective

- I know what makes me and others feel happy

Settling-down poem

> 'Here are my ears, I can hear,
> Here are my eyes, I can see,
> Here is my heart, I can feel,
> Here is my friend, next to me,
> I am ready to learn and play,
> I'm sitting down, legs crossed, hooray!'

Warm-up game

As a group, sing the song 'If You're Happy and You Know It' with the children, and include lots of different actions that you can do if you are feeling happy. Once you have focused on the feeling 'happy', change the song to focus on

38 Emotions

other feelings such as 'sad' and 'angry', and accompany the singing with actions that you would do if you were feeling that way. Some examples of the actions that you could do are as follows:

- Happy: jump for joy, clap your hands, and, give a high-five.
- Sad: have a cry, slump your shoulders, and, give a sigh.
- Angry: clench your fists, stamp your feet, and, give a shout.

Main activity

Before the start of this session, look through old magazines and newspapers and cut out pictures of people, or animals, or of a variety of characters, all expressing different emotions.

When you come together with the children, draw a happy face on one large piece of sugar paper or card and ask the children what feeling the face is showing. Then lay out all the pictures that you have cut out beforehand and ask them to pick out the ones that show characters feeling happy, which they can then stick down on to the piece of sugar paper. As you are doing this together, talk to the children about how they can tell when others are feeling happy, such as looking at their facial expressions or body posture, listening to what they say, or observing how they behave.

The next part of this activity is to play a game with the children. Get lots of small plastic balls of the same colour and spread these out all over the floor. Give each child a container (e.g. a small bowl or bag) and they have to rush around and collect these balls, but every time they pick one up, they have to tell the group one thing that makes them feel happy. Once they have done this, they can then keep the balls in their container. Let the children play this game for some time (e.g. ten minutes) and when you say 'stop', they have to sit in the circle and count their balls; the winner is the one who managed to collect the most.

Relaxation

Have a variety of photographs or pictures of different peaceful scenes (e.g. a snowy landscape, a beautiful mountain, a relaxing forest, some cuddly animals, a Christmas scene, etc.), and ask the children to pick one picture that makes them feel happy and calm. Encourage the children to look at their picture carefully, taking in all the detail. They then have to close their eyes and try and recreate this peaceful picture in their minds. With their eyes closed and whilst visualising their peaceful scene, ask the children to think about what they can see, what they can hear and smell, what they might be able to taste, and who is there with them. After a few minutes, the children can open their eyes and look at their picture again. Let the children know that when they are in a difficult or unsettling situation, they can always close their eyes and think of their peaceful picture, trying to recreate it in their minds, which should help them to feel calm.

Resources

- Settling-down poem and music (if needed)
- Pictures cut out from magazines and newspapers
- One large piece of sugar paper
- Coloured pens or markers
- Glue sticks
- Small balls of the same colour
- Small containers for each child (e.g. small bowl, bag)
- Pictures and photographs of peaceful scenery
- Homework books

Homework

The children need to find one picture from an old magazine of someone feeling happy. They then cut this out and stick it on to a blank page in their homework books. The children will need to think of things that make them feel happy and will need to record these on the page with the happy picture. They can choose to cut out more pictures from magazines or draw pictures of the things that make them feel happy.

Session 4

Learning objective

- I know what makes me and others feel sad

Settling-down poem

'Here are my ears, I can hear,
Here are my eyes, I can see,
Here is my heart, I can feel,
Here is my friend, next to me,
I am ready to learn and play,
I'm sitting down, legs crossed, hooray!'

Warm-up game

Before the start of the session, get a number of paper plates and cut them in half so that one half can be the top of a head with eyes and eyebrows, and the other half can be the bottom of the head with a nose and mouth. Using marker pens, draw these facial features on each half of the plates; the features have to convey different expressions of feelings, such as a smiley mouth corresponding with happy eyes and eyebrows, a sad mouth corresponding with sad eyes and

40 Emotions

eyebrows, etc. Once you have done this, stick an ice-cream stick to the back of each half-plate. The activity with the children is for each one to choose a half-plate and hold it up to their face so that the rest of the group need to guess what the feeling might be. The child will have to alter their own expressions in order to correspond with the part of the expression on the plate halves that they have chosen. Allow the children to have several turns each at choosing a half-plate and changing their facial expressions to convey different feelings.

Main activity

This activity is the same as the one from the previous session, but this time, it focuses on the emotion of feeling sad. Make sure to have the rest of the pictures of people, animals, or characters left over from the previous session, showing different emotions.

When you come together with the children, draw a sad face on one large piece of sugar paper or card, and ask the children what feeling the face is showing. Then lay out all the pictures that you have and ask them to pick out the ones that show characters feeling sad, which they can then stick down on to the piece of sugar paper. As you are doing this together, talk to the children about how they can tell when others are feeling sad, such as looking at their facial expressions or body posture, listening to what they say, or observing how they behave.

The next part of this activity is to play a game with the children. Get lots of small plastic balls of the same colour and spread these out all over the floor. Give each child a container (e.g. a small bowl or bag), and they have to rush around and collect these balls, but every time they pick one up, they have to tell the group one thing that makes them sad. Once they have done this, they can then keep the balls in their container. Let the children play this game for some time (e.g. ten minutes) and when you say 'stop', they have to sit in the circle and count their balls; the winner is the one who managed to collect the most.

Relaxation

This activity will involve you making some rainbow beans before the session, in order to create a sensory relaxation experience for the children. Find some light coloured beans such as lima, white, or pinto beans, and get a variety of different food colouring. Use one cup of beans to 15 drops of colouring, and shake these well in sealable bags until the beans are fully coated. Lay the beans out on paper towels or tin foil, with each of the different colours laid out separately so that they can dry out. Once the beans are dry, place them in different trays made of different materials such as tin, metal, wood, paper, and plastic. The activity will involve the children playing with the beans within each tray, moving them around with their hands whilst looking at the colours and listening to the sounds that they make. If you would like, you can add different scents to each different colour so that the children can also smell each scent as they play. They should do this without speaking to each other and whilst relaxing music is playing in the background.

Resources

- Settling-down poem and music (if needed)
- Paper plates
- Coloured pens or markers
- Scissors and sticky tape
- Ice-cream sticks
- Pictures cut out from magazines and newspapers
- One large piece of sugar paper
- Glue sticks
- Small balls of the same colour
- Small containers for each child (e.g. small bowl, bag)
- Light coloured beans
- Food colouring
- Essential oils or scents
- Sealable or zip-lock bags
- Paper towels or tin foil
- Trays made of different materials
- Relaxing music
- Homework books

Homework

The children need to find one picture from a magazine of someone feeling sad. They then cut this out and stick it on to a blank page in their homework books. The children will need to think of things that make them feel sad and will need to record these on the page with the sad picture. They can choose to cut out more pictures from magazines or draw pictures of the things that make them feel sad.

Session 5

Learning objective

- I know when I am feeling angry

Settling-down poem

*'Here are my ears, I can hear,
Here are my eyes, I can see,
Here is my heart, I can feel,
Here is my friend, next to me,
I am ready to learn and play,
I'm sitting down, legs crossed, hooray!'*

Warm-up game

You need four pictures showing four different emotions (happy, sad, excited, and angry), and then place these in four different envelopes. Jumble them up and then put one envelope in each corner of the room. Tell the children to move to one corner, open the envelope to reveal the picture, but to not tell you what it is. They will have to act out the feeling using only gestures and their bodies (no words), and you need to try and guess what feeling they are acting out. When they have done this for one corner and you have guessed correctly, ask them to move on to the next corner and carry on with the game until they have been in all four corners of the room. If you guess a feeling incorrectly though, you have to do something silly for the children such as doing a funny dance.

Main activity

Get two or three large pieces of sugar paper or card and tape these together to make one long piece of paper. Choose one child from the group to lie down on top of this piece of paper and you can draw around them to create a body outline. Have a few pictures of people or characters looking angry or expressing anger for the children to look at to support their thinking, and then ask them how they might feel and how their bodies might change when they feel are feeling angry. Some examples of these are: they stamp their **feet**, they clench their **teeth** and **fists**, their **forehead** feels hot, their **hands** get sweaty, their **heart** begins to race, they use their **mouth** to start shouting, etc. As you identify what begins to happen to your body, ask the children to use a coloured marker and to draw or colour in on the body outline, the different parts of the body that gets affected when they become angry.

Relaxation

This activity involves using bubbles to help the children relax and feel calm. You can either buy small bottles of bubble mixture for each child, or you can make your own. You can do this by mixing washing-up liquid or shampoo with water, and then adding a little bit of sugar to help thicken the mixture. Stir the mixture gently and then test it out to see whether it will create bubbles, or whether it might need more soap, etc. You can use a variety of recyclable materials to create bubble blowers such as pipe cleaners, straws, top ends of plastic bottles, and string.

Give each child some bubble mixture and a blower, and then ask them to blow bubbles by doing the following: thinking of something that worries them or makes them feel scared or angry, taking a deep breath in, and then blowing out all of these difficult feelings as they breathe out to make each bubble. They can then sit and watch their bubbles float away, which can also reflect their feelings and worries being blown away and disappearing.

Resources

- Settling-down poem and music (if needed)
- Four pictures of different feelings (happy, sad, excited, angry) and four envelopes
- Three large pieces of sugar paper or card
- Sticky tape and scissors
- Pens, pencils, and coloured markers
- Bottles for blowing bubbles or ingredients for making your own bubble mixture and blowers, for example:
    - Bubble mixture: bowls, spoons, water, sugar, washing-up liquid, or shampoo
    - Bubble blowers: plastic bottles, string, pipe cleaners, and straws
- Homework books

Homework

With adult support, the children need to draw an outline of a body in their homework books and then with coloured pens, draw or colour in the parts of the body that change when they start feeling angry, just as they have done in the session. If they become angry before the next session, they then need to record in their books what happened or what made them feel angry, so that they can then share this with the group in the next session.

Session 6

Learning objective

- I know what makes me feel angry

Settling-down poem

> 'Here are my ears, I can hear,
> Here are my eyes, I can see,

44   Emotions

Here is my heart, I can feel,
Here is my friend, next to me,
I am ready to learn and play,
I'm sitting down, legs crossed, hooray!'

Warm-up game

Before the start of the session, look through a variety of old magazines so that you can cut out pictures of large individual eyes, ears, noses, and mouths, so that these are available for the children to use. Then, have individual pieces of paper, one for each child, with an oval face shape drawn in the middle of each page. The task is for the children to choose whichever combination of eyes, ears, noses, and mouths that they want and stick them down on the oval shape to create silly faces. They can then decorate their faces by adding in more features or colours, to create things such as their hair, jewellery, or clothes.

Main activity

Have the large body outline from the previous session available for the children to see. Encourage them to look through their homework books and check if there are any areas that they coloured in at home that is not coloured in on their group body outline, and if there are, they then need to use markers to colour in or draw all the parts of their body that can become affected when they get angry. An extension of this activity is for the children to volunteer what kinds of things make them feel angry, which they can record on small pieces of paper as drawings or words. You can then take all of these pieces of paper and stick them on the outside of the body outline. They can also volunteer what situations or events they have noticed that make others around them feel angry (e.g. parents, siblings, friends, teachers, etc.), and again add these to the outside of the body outline as drawings and captions on pieces of paper. This represents how things outside of ourselves can lead to how our bodies feel, and how we then also feel on the inside.

Relaxation

The children are going to practice some elephant breathing; they stand with their arms to their sides and as they breathe in deeply, they raise their arms in the air like an elephant trunk. As they breathe out, they then slowly lower their arms back down. Do this with the children a few times so that they can practise their breathing, whilst relaxing music is playing in the background.

Resources

- Settling-down poem and music (if needed)
- Pictures of eyes, ears, noses, and mouths
- Piece of paper for each child with oval shape drawn in the centre

Emotions   45

- Coloured markers and pens, and glue sticks
- Large body outline from the previous session
- Small pieces of paper
- Relaxing music
- Homework books

Homework

In their homework books, the children need to draw pictures of the things that they know make them feel angry. They will also need to extend this by observing those around them and recording what they have noticed that makes others feel angry.

Session 7

Learning objective

- I know how to make myself feel better

Settling-down poem

*'Here are my ears, I can hear,
Here are my eyes, I can see,
Here is my heart, I can feel,
Here is my friend, next to me,
I am ready to learn and play,
I'm sitting down, legs crossed, hooray!'*

Warm-up game

Using a variety of fun and quick-paced songs, get the children to dance around the room until the music stops. When the music stops, they have to freeze in whichever position they were in, and then try not to move at all until the music comes back on. As an extension to this game, when the music stops, you have to ask the children to freeze into specific shapes and positions such as letters, shapes, or animals, etc.

Main activity

This activity aims to help the children begin to explore what kind of things might help them feel better when they are angry or finding situations tricky. Have lots of pictures, photographs, and relevant books about being helpful, and kind, etc. all over the floor for the children to look at and get ideas of things that could be helpful to help them feel calmer. Some examples of these are breathing exercises, counting to five, hugging someone, giving someone a cupcake, drawing someone a picture, playing with play dough, reading a story, etc. When the children find something that they feel is going to be helpful for them, they then need to record it as a drawing or word, with your support, on individual pieces of coloured paper.

Relaxation

This relaxation activity will link into the main game and will extend the exploration into ways that children can feel better when they are angry. Have a variety of objects and materials available that are calming in nature, such as soft cushions, teddy bears, squeezy toys, play dough, story books, dry scented rice, etc. Using a fast-paced, loud, and thundery piece of music (e.g. an emotional classic music piece such as 'Night on Bald Mountain' by Modest Mussorgsky), get the children to think of something that has made them angry recently and then act out an 'angry dance' to the music. Then, by shaking a musical instrument (e.g. bells or a tambourine), you then prompt the children to stop dancing and to move around to the different objects and materials that you have made available for them. They then interact with these, one at a time, to explore which one of them helped them feel better and calmer. Let the children try all the different materials and then tell each other which one they preferred to help them feel better.

Resources

- Settling-down poem and music (if needed)
- A variety of fun and fast-paced songs
- Pictures, photographs and books that highlight ways of feeling better
- Small pieces of coloured paper
- Pencils and coloured pens
- Calming materials and objects (e.g. cushions, squeezy toys, play dough, scented dry rice, teddies, picture books, etc.)
- 'Angry' piece of music
- Bells or tambourine
- Homework books

Homework

Let the children take home a variety of colourful pieces of paper and with support from their parents, explore more ways that could be helpful in order to make them feel better (e.g. going for a walk, running around, having a sleep, etc.). They then record these as drawings and words on their individual pieces of paper, and then stick these into their homework books.

Session 8

Learning objective

- I know how to make others feel better

Settling-down poem

'Here are my ears, I can hear,
Here are my eyes, I can see,
Here is my heart, I can feel,
Here is my friend, next to me,
I am ready to learn and play,
I'm sitting down, legs crossed, hooray!'

Warm-up game

Before the beginning of the session, look through old magazines or the internet, and either cut or print out pictures of people, animals, or characters feeling happy, sad, and angry. Then, hide these pictures around the room for the children to find and lay three hoops on the floor: one with a picture of a happy face, one with a picture of a sad face, and one with a picture of an angry face. The children have to try and find the pictures that you have hidden and then place each in their correct feelings hoop. When all the pictures have been found and sorted, talk to the children about how they knew which picture would go in which hoop.

Main activity

This activity is an extension of the one from the previous session and aims to help children begin to explore what kind of things might help others feel better when they are angry or finding situations tricky. Firstly, you will need a colourful box that you can call the 'Helpful Heroes' box, and explain to the children that they are all going to learn how to become 'Helpful Heroes'. Their task is to work together and decide on ways that people can help each other to feel better. As in the previous session, have lots of pictures, photographs, and relevant books about being helpful, and kind, etc. all over the floor for the children to look at and get ideas of things that could be helpful; for example, breathing exercises, counting to five, hugging someone, giving someone a cupcake, drawing someone a picture, etc. When the children find something that they feel is going to be helpful to others, they then need to record it as a drawing or words, with your support, on individual pieces of coloured paper. Once they have recorded each idea on one piece of paper, they pop it into the 'Helpful Heroes' box and go off to try and find some more ideas. This box could be added to over time and could be kept in a central location in the classroom so that children can go to it for some ideas when either they or a friend is feeling angry or finding it difficult to cope.

Relaxation

Have a variety of pieces of paper or material with different textures such as corrugated, rough, sandy, furry, spiky, soft, hard, glossy, etc. The children close

48 Emotions

their eyes and you pass them a piece of material or paper to hold and feel with their fingers, and they then have to try and describe what they are feeling, and where they can remember or imagine feeling the same texture. For example:

- Corrugated texture on a fence near their house.
- Sandy texture when they were last at the beach.
- Furry texture on their favourite teddy bear.
- Soft texture on their warm blanket in bed.
- Glossy texture on the whiteboard in class.

Let the children feel all the different textures that you have, but always with their eyes closed and with relaxing music playing in the background.

Resources

- Settling-down poem and music (if needed)
- Pictures of people, animals, or characters feeling happy, sad, and angry
- Three hoops and three emotions faces: happy, sad, and angry
- Pictures, photographs and books that highlight ways of feeling better
- Small pieces of coloured paper
- Pencils and coloured pens
- 'Helpful Heroes' box
- Textured pieces of paper and material
- Relaxing music
- Homework books

Homework

Let the children take home a variety of colourful pieces of paper so that they can ask their parents, family, and friends about ways that they find helpful to calm them down. They then record these as drawings and words, with support, on their individual pieces of paper. The children can then decide whether they want to stick their pieces of paper in their homework books or whether they want to take them in to school and place them in the 'Helpful Heroes' box. They could even create their own box at home with strategies that they have explored with their family and friends.

Emotions 49

Section 5 – Awareness

From a very young age, children begin to develop a sense of self and to see themselves from the viewpoint of others around them. This is known as self-awareness, where they start to become their own person and begin to find out about themselves, such as that first peek they take at the mirror when they realise that they are actually looking at themselves. Over time, children begin to work out that they are separate beings from other people that they know and encounter, initially in the way that they look, and then extending this knowledge to how they think and feel.

Young children display self-awareness in the way that they understand and use self-referring language such as 'I', 'me', 'my', and 'mine'. When children become self-aware, they work out and are clearly able to express what they like and do not like, what their needs might be, as well as starting to recognise their unique habits, traits, and behaviours. They also begin to demonstrate emotions linked to feeling self-conscious such as pride in an accomplishment, guilt or embarrassment, or determination to make amends when they have made an inappropriate choice. They begin to understand their actions and make judgements about their own strengths and achievements, and can therefore start to make decisions about what they want to do as well as what they might want to get better at doing. At this point, they can also start adopting beliefs about themselves that can be positive in terms of recognising their talents and skills, or which can be negative in terms of viewing themselves as lacking in ability and not being able to do what others around them can do.

As they get older, children develop an awareness of the link between their thoughts and their feelings, and they begin to understand how what they think and feel at any given moment will affect what they do and how they can respond to others. When children begin to develop their understanding of how they think, feel, and act, they are better able to reflect on how they learn and problem-solve. The development of self-awareness is therefore linked to metacognition, which at its most basic is 'thinking about thinking'. This means that they start to understand and regulate their thinking processes in order to support their social development and their behavioural responses. They build their awareness of how they acquire knowledge and are able to reflect on how they learn, which enables them to maximise their learning potential. They begin to see how their strengths can affect how they execute and accomplish different tasks, as well as how any area of weakness can have an effect on their learning and achievement.

Self-awareness allows children to recognise their strengths and qualities, and what makes them unique to everyone else. Furthermore, self-awareness is an executive function, which means that it is a skill that children will use to organise and use information effectively. It enables the development of skills for monitoring and regulating their behaviour, and for being flexible thinkers and adapting what they know, which will thus optimise their ability to learn.

Being self-aware not only involves children being able to tune into their own feelings, but also being able to recognise and understand the needs, feelings, and behaviour of others. They are able to make connections between how their own feelings and behaviour can impact on those around them, and therefore develop their ability to adapt and respond more appropriately in varying situations. This means that being self-aware will positively affect their understanding, their behaviour, and their ability to reflect on what they and others are feeling and doing. This in turn has an impact on the development of meaningful relationships and their ability to care for and empathise with others.

Self-awareness is a critical higher-order thinking process that allows children to monitor, adjust, and control their behaviour, and to amend their perceptions and belief about themselves and the world around them. They learn from the way they experience the world and their interactions within it, which encourages adaptability and flexibility as they work their way through challenges and new learning opportunities. This enables them to build further skills and connections in areas such as creativity, resourcefulness, inquisitiveness, and resilience, and thus supports them to develop their social and emotional ability, as well as enable them to reach their full potential.

Although all of the areas covered in this programme contribute to the development of self-awareness, the activities in this section focus specifically on children being able to demonstrate knowledge about themselves such as their likes and dislikes, and beginning to identify what is unique and special about them. This includes the ability to notice and be aware of what makes them similar and different to others around them. The sessions further aim to support children to consider the choices that they can make in terms of how each of their choices can affect them and others in different ways, as well as thinking about how to make amends when an inappropriate choice has been made, and how to show care towards others.

52 Awareness

Session 1

Learning objective

- I know things about me such as what I look like

Settling-down poem

*'Here are my ears, I can hear,
Here are my eyes, I can see,
Here is my heart, I can feel,
Here is my friend, next to me,
I am ready to learn and play,
I'm sitting down, legs crossed, hooray!'*

Warm-up game

Before the session starts, find a variety of simple pictures in old magazines or from the internet (e.g. a dog, flower, car, tree, or castle), and cut or print these out. Then, find an A4 piece of card and cut a small circle into the middle of it.

At the beginning of this activity, hold up one of the pictures that you have found, but cover it with the piece of card so that the children can only see part of the picture through the small circle in the card. Ask the children to try and guess what the picture might be from what they can see, but if they are unable to do so initially, move the circle around the picture slowly to enable them to see different parts of it. As soon as they guess what the picture is correctly, remove the card and show them the whole picture. Once you have done this with one picture, move on to the other pictures that you have found, continuing to present them in the same way until the children are able to guess what all of them are.

Main activity

Before the start of the session, prepare a large piece of card for each child by dividing it into eight different sections. Label each section with the following headings:

- Me
- My age, or, My birthday
- My family
- My house
- My friends
- My favourite food
- My favourite game
- My favourite colour

In order to support the children with this activity, have a variety of old magazines from which they can cut out pictures, as well as different pictures printed off the internet, and craft materials that they can also use. These resources will help them to start working on their individual pieces of card, in order to create their very own 'All About Me' posters. Make sure to explain to the children what the different sections on their cards are, and they can then start adding in both pictures and drawings to represent important information about themselves. The children can start on these posters during this activity but will then need to take them home and finish them for homework.

Relaxation

This activity will involve you and the children creating some sensory salt together. Allow each child to take a cupful of some fine salt and then pour this into their own sealable bags. They then choose what colour and scent that they want their salt to be by adding a few drops of their chosen food colouring and their favourite scent (e.g. vanilla, lavender, almond, etc.) to their salt packets. They then seal their bags and shake them vigorously to mix everything together, and once their salt is fully coated, they can then pour it out into their own individual trays. They can then play with their salt by using their fingers or using different materials to do different things to it such as drawing patterns in

54 Awareness

their salt with a fork, blowing it gently with a straw, or shifting it from side to side to hear the noise that it makes in the tray. Have some relaxing music playing in the background while the children are doing this.

Resources

- Settling-down poem and music (if needed)
- Variety of simple pictures
- A4 piece of card with small circle cut into it
- One large piece of card for each child, divided into eight sections, and labelled
- Old magazines
- Pictures downloaded from the internet
- Art and craft materials
- Coloured pens and pencils
- Scissors and glue
- Fine salt
- Cups
- Sealable or zip-lock bags
- Food colouring
- Varied scents or essences
- One tray for each child
- Relaxing music
- Homework books

Homework

The children have to take the 'All About Me' posters home that they have started creating during the session, and they can then finish this with support from their family, for homework. They can also add photographs to their posters and decorate them in whichever way that they want.

Session 2

Learning objective

- I know what is special about me

Settling-down poem

> 'Here are my ears, I can hear,
> Here are my eyes, I can see,
> Here is my heart, I can feel,
> Here is my friend, next to me,
> I am ready to learn and play,
> I'm sitting down, legs crossed, hooray!'

Warm-up game

Give each child three large pieces of paper and three different coloured crayons. This task will be where they take their 'crayons for a walk' by first using one piece of paper and one crayon, and then moving the crayon around the page in any pattern that they want. The second part is using the second piece of paper and moving two crayons at once around the page, and the third part is using the third piece of paper and moving three crayons at once around the page. Once all of the children have done this, ask them to swap their papers with each other and to then look carefully at each other's patterns to see if they remind them of anything (e.g. can they see any characters or shapes in each other's drawings?).

Main activity

Before the start of the session, gather a bag full of objects that could be considered mundane (for example: paper, wool, pencil, tissue, a plastic cup, etc.), as well as those that could be considered special (e.g. a photograph, key, necklace, watch, a keyring, etc.). You will also need a plastic bowl and a special box such as a treasure chest. The task to carry out with the children is to tell them that special objects go into the treasure chest and the others that are not so special go into the plastic bowl. They can then take turns to pick out an object from the bag and then sort them into the chest or the bowl.

The next part of the activity is to read a story to the children about what makes people special and unique such as the following books:

- *I'm the Best* by Lucy Cousins
- *What I Like About Me* by Allia Zobel-Nolan
- *I'm Special, I'm Me* by Ann Meek
- *Marvelous Me, Inside and Out* by Lisa Bullard

Once you have read a special story to the children, give out small pieces of paper and ask them what they think is special and unique about them, which they can then draw on the individual pieces of paper. They can then show the rest of the group what they have drawn about themselves, and then place their pieces of paper in the treasure chest to represent that what they have to offer is just as special as the items that are already in the chest.

Relaxation

Let the children use the crayon creations that they made in the warm-up activity when they took their crayons for a walk. They can choose the drawing that they want and then using colouring pencils and crayons, they then quietly sit and colour in between the lines and patterns that they have done, while listening to relaxing music.

Resources

- Settling-down poem and music (if needed)
- Three large pieces of paper per child
- Lots of crayons
- Bag of mundane and special objects
- Plastic bowl and special box (e.g. treasure chest)
- Picture story books
- Small pieces of paper
- Pens and pencils
- Relaxing music
- Homework books

Homework

Give the children some small pieces of paper such as the ones that they used during the main activity, so that they can draw individual pictures on each piece about the things that they feel make them special and unique. Their family can help them to do this task and they can then stick down the pictures in their homework books with labels or captions.

Session 3

Learning objective

- I know what I like and what I don't like

Settling-down poem

> 'Here are my ears, I can hear,
> Here are my eyes, I can see,
> Here is my heart, I can feel,
> Here is my friend, next to me,
> I am ready to learn and play,
> I'm sitting down, legs crossed, hooray!'

Warm-up game

Give a small ball to one child who starts off the game by saying, 'My name is …' and then rolling it to the next child who says, 'Your name is … and my name is …'. Go round the group and when all the children have had a go, do an action sequence that everyone has to follow (e.g. touch your nose, roll your eyes, tickle your ears, pull out your tongue, and stamp your feet). Then have a second round where the children roll the ball to one another and complete the sentence 'I like …', and once everyone has had a go, do the same action sequence as in the first round, but try and do it much quicker. They then have a third round where the children roll the ball and complete the sentence 'I don't like . . .', and at the end, they carry out the same action sequence as quickly as they can.

Main activity

Introduce the children to a puppet or toy of your choice such as a large teddy bear. The children take turns to pass the teddy around and when they are holding it, they can tell it about one thing that they like. Do this twice so that each child can say two things that they like, and then go around once more and see if the children can remember and say something that someone else in the group likes. Then do the same activity where the children initially tell the teddy two things that they do not like, and then try and remember something that they heard someone else in the group say that they do not like.

The next part of the activity is to get the children to interact and engage in different actions when you offer a specific statement related to their likes and dislikes. For example, you can use action statements such as:

- Jump up if you like dogs.
- Clap your hands if you like ice cream.
- Shake hands with a friend who also likes ice cream.
- Wiggle your bottom if you like snow.
- Stamp your feet if you don't like fighting.
- Dance around if you don't like thunder.
- Tap on a chair if you don't like porridge.
- Wave to a friend if you don't like football.

Relaxation

This activity is a relaxation exercise that helps children to begin focusing on their breathing to help them feel calm and relaxed. Ask the children to place their hands in the space just above their tummies and then to practice breathing in slowly and deeply. Focus their attention on how they can see and feel their tummies going up and down as they breathe in and out. Ask the children to breathe in for a count of five, hold for another count of five, and then breathe out for a count of eight. Do this two or three times until the children feel calm and relaxed, and if you want, you could have relaxing music playing in the background.

Resources
- Settling-down poem and music (if needed)
- Small ball
- Puppet or teddy bear
- Relaxing music
- Homework books

58 Awareness

Homework

In their homework books, the children need to write or draw pictures of the things that they like and do not like when they are at home or away from school. They also need to spend some time with their family to find out what they like and do not like, and together they can also record these as drawings or words in their books.

Session 4

Learning objective

- I know how we are the same and different

Settling-down poem

> 'Here are my ears, I can hear,
> Here are my eyes, I can see,
> Here is my heart, I can feel,
> Here is my friend, next to me,
> I am ready to learn and play,
> I'm sitting down, legs crossed, hooray!'

Warm-up game

This game involves the children observing each other closely and noticing things about each other, which will link to the main activity in this session. Give the group a chance to look at each other carefully first and then choose one child that you take away from the group and change something about them (e.g. the child takes his shoes off, or puts on a scarf, or wears his top back to front, or puts on a moustache, etc.). You both then re-join the group and the other children have to work out and volunteer what is different about the child that went out of the room with you. Make sure that everyone has a turn at being able to change something about themselves at least once during this game.

Main activity

Use objects or toys that have similarities and differences when you compare them to each other, such as pairs of socks or sorting bears. The children can then spend some time putting these together according to their similarities (e.g. by colour, shape, or their patterns), and then also highlighting what the differences about them might be.

Extend this activity by giving a child a ball and ask them to roll it to a peer according to a specific descriptive phrase that you offer them, such as 'Roll the ball to a girl' or 'Roll the ball to someone who is in your class'. Make sure to increase the complexity of these phrases during the activity so that the children have to really listen, observe, and make choices about who they roll the ball to. Some examples of these phrases might be:

- Roll the ball to someone who has got brown hair and likes football.
- Roll the ball to someone who has a sister and who can speak more than one language.
- Roll the ball to someone who likes ice cream and is a good friend.
- Roll the ball to someone who is a girl who has a sister and brown hair.
- Roll the ball to someone who is wearing green socks and who has a dog and blue eyes.

Use these phrases to highlight to the children how they are similar and how they are different from each other.

Relaxation

This activity works best if you have some calm and relaxing music playing in the background. It is used to help the children relax by loosening different parts of their bodies. Make sure to model this sequence of movements for the children to copy you as you move through the activity.

- While you are sitting on the floor, rotate your shoulders forward and back, and then move your head and neck in circular movements, to the left and then the right.
- Stretch your arms up over your head as high as they can go and while they are in the air, stretch out your fingers and then roll them into a fist. Do this a few times and then bring your arms down slowly.
- Move on to bringing your knees up to your chest and then stretching out your legs in front of you. With legs stretched out, point your toes out as far as they will go, and then curl them up. Do this a few times and then bring your knees back to your chest.
- Rest your head on your knees and hug your legs, closing your eyes, and listening to the music for a few minutes.

Resources
- Settling-down poem and music (if needed)
- Objects for children to wear during warm-up game (e.g. scarf, hat, glasses, coat, etc.)
- Toys or objects that have similarities and differences (e.g. pairing socks, sorting bears, shapes, etc.)
- Small ball
- Relaxing music
- Homework books

60   Awareness

Homework

The children need to carry out an investigation at home with the help of a parent. They need to observe their family and friends carefully, and in their homework books note down in pictures or words, what similarities and differences that they can see in them (for example: their hair and eye colour, height, clothes, what they like and do not like, etc.).

Session 5

Learning objective

- I know that I can make good choices

Settling-down poem

'Here are my ears, I can hear,
Here are my eyes, I can see,
Here is my heart, I can feel,
Here is my friend, next to me,
I am ready to learn and play,
I'm sitting down, legs crossed, hooray!'

Warm-up game

Before the start of the session, find a black and white outline of a butterfly that you can photocopy so that every child has a copy of their own. When each child has their own butterfly, they need to listen to an instruction that you give out that will involve a choice that they will have to make, for example:

- Colour the right wing in a blue or red crayon, you choose.
- Use a cotton ball or a pom-pom for the butterfly's head, you choose.
- Stick on some sequins or some glitter on the body, you choose.

Make sure that the children colour in and decorate their butterflies in the ways that they choose and then support them to cut their butterflies out as they will need them for the relaxation activity.

Main activity

Introduce the children to two puppets; one is good and kind and the other is cheeky and naughty. Then, tell the children a short story scenario that presents a choice to the children. Before the children can offer their own ideas, the 'good' puppet tells the group what a positive choice might be and the 'naughty' puppet tells the group a negative choice. The children can then decide which puppet they would choose for the story to have the best outcome. Once you have done this for one story scenario, use a few more to continue this activity on with the children.

Some example scenarios for this activity could be:

- There was a new boy at school who wanted to make some friends.
    - Choice 1 – He went up to some children at playtime and asked them to play.
    - Choice 2 – He was silly in class to get everyone to laugh and got into trouble.
- The girl wanted to get a new doll that she saw in the shop.
    - Choice 1 – She asked her Mum if she could buy it for her birthday.
    - Choice 2 – She shouted and screamed at her Mum to get it now.

Relaxation

Using the butterflies from the warm-up activity, the children then have to try and balance their own butterfly on their noses. In order to do this, they need to stay very still and really focus on their breathing. Let the children try this by standing up first, then sitting down, and then lying down to see which position they find easier to balance their butterfly without it falling off their nose. Let the children do this while listening to relaxing music playing in the background.

Resources

- Settling-down poem and music (if needed)
- Copies of butterfly outlines
- Colouring pencils and crayons

- Craft materials (e.g. pom-poms, cotton balls, glitter, sequins, tissue paper, etc.)
- Scissors and glue
- Two puppets
- Relaxing music
- Homework books

Homework

Ask the children to draw two pictures in their homework books of the two puppets that were used in the session, making sure to draw each one on different pages. Then, with their family's support, they have to observe what others around them do and try and work out if anything they saw was a positive or a negative choice. They can then record what they have noticed as drawings in their books, on whichever page corresponds to the puppet and choice that was made. The children will need some support to do this as a way of getting them to begin to notice the kinds of choices that others around them are making.

Session 6

Learning objective

- I know what to do if I haven't made a good choice

Settling-down poem

'Here are my ears, I can hear,
Here are my eyes, I can see,
Here is my heart, I can feel,
Here is my friend, next to me,
I am ready to learn and play,
I'm sitting down, legs crossed, hooray!'

Warm-up game

Before the start of the session, take some masking tape and use it to draw a few different shapes on the floor, for example, a square, a triangle, a star, a heart, and a circle. These shapes aim to involve the children in listening and following a variety of instructions that will become more complex as the activity progresses. The first step of the activity is to give the children a simple instruction such as:

- Walk to the heart.
- Walk to the triangle.
- Walk to the square.

The second part of the activity is to offer the children more difficult instructions such as:

- Crawl to the circle.
- Hop to the square.
- Frog-leap to the star.

The third part of the activity is to offer the children more complex two-step instructions such as:

- Walk to the heart and then hop to the square.
- Crawl to the circle but without touching the star.
- Jump to the triangle but go round the heart first.

Main activity

For this activity, you will need to use the two puppets from the previous session who will continue to offer both a positive and a negative choice. You start off the session by offering the children a scenario, and then each of the puppets offer their choices to the children, but this time, they choose one child to hold one puppet and represent its choice, and a second child to hold the other puppet and represent the second choice. The child holding the puppet that offers the positive choice then needs to explain what the consequence of that choice might be, and the child holding the puppet that offers the negative choice needs to explain the consequence of making that choice. When the consequence of a negative choice is identified, then the rest of the group need to help the child decide on what they could do to make amends. The children may need some support to help them to do this, such as having pictures available as prompts for possible strategies that they could suggest. Some examples scenarios are outlined here:

Scenario	Choices	Consequences	Amends
My sister wants me to play with her but I don't want to.	Positive – I tell her I'll play with her tomorrow.	She says okay and we play together tomorrow.	I give her a hug. I say sorry to her. I play with her.
	Negative – I shout at her so she will leave me alone.	She starts crying and tells Mum, and I get into trouble.	
My friend is mean to me and tells me to go away.	Positive – I find someone else to play with.	I have lots of fun with my other friends.	I say sorry to him.
	Negative – I hit him because he's mean.	I get into trouble with my teacher.	I tell him I want to play with someone else too.

64   Awareness

Relaxation

The children need to play the 'Copy My Breathing' game where you have to model different types of breathing such as deep breathing and counting your breaths, alongside doing varied actions, which the children have to copy. The actions should be slow and focused such as raising and lowering your arms, making a lying-down figure-of-eight with your fingers, raising one knee and then the other, etc. Have some relaxing music playing in the background while the children carry out these actions.

Resources

- Settling-down poem and music (if needed)
- Masking tape
- Two puppets
- Picture prompts (if needed)
- Relaxing music
- Homework books

Homework

The children have to observe others around them and try and identify times when they have made the incorrect choice, and then try and identify what they did to make amends. This might be difficult for some of the children to spot so they could be supported to do this activity by sitting down with their parents and asking them when they have made a negative choice and what they did to make it better. The children can then draw pictures of these strategies in their homework books and with help, label what they have drawn.

Session 7

Learning objective

- I know how my choices can affect others

Settling-down poem

> 'Here are my ears, I can hear,
> Here are my eyes, I can see,
> Here is my heart, I can feel,
> Here is my friend, next to me,
> I am ready to learn and play,
> I'm sitting down, legs crossed, hooray!'

Warm-up game

Put the children in pairs so that they can play the 'Mirror Me' game with each other. One child starts by making any action that they want with their bodies and faces, and their partner has to copy what they are doing. After around one minute, they change roles so that the other child has a chance to make the actions for their partner to copy. The final part of this activity is for each pair to do this while the rest of the group watches so that they can decide who the best 'action-maker' is and who is the best 'action-copier' in the group.

Main activity

Before the start of the session, you will need to prepare some scenarios and choices on individual cards. Use some of the scenarios that you have worked on with the children during the past two sessions as well as one or two new ones to challenge their thinking. Write each scenario on individual large pieces of paper and make sure to include a drawing to serve as a prompt for the children who may not be able to read the scenario. Then write down the corresponding positive and negative choices for that scenario on their own individual pieces of paper. You will also need to prepare some large red circles and green hearts, which you can cut out from pieces of card.

The activity starts by you putting one scenario on the floor, and then placing near it the two corresponding choice cards. Choose two children from the group and give each their own bean bag; they then have to throw their bag so that it lands on (or as close to) one of the choices. Once their bean bag lands on one of the choices, the children then have to volunteer ideas of how that choice might have affected those involved. For example, if a positive choice was to play a game that someone else wanted to play, then this would make the other person happy. If a negative choice was to push someone because they were annoying, then this would make the other person sad and possibly scared. If the children offer a positive effect (such as making someone happy), then you can record this as a short phrase and a simple drawing on a green heart card, and if the children offer a negative effect (such as making someone sad), then you record this on a red circle.

The final part of this activity is to give the children some small red circles and green hearts of their own so that they can draw their own pictures of the effects that they talked about during the session. They can then stick these down in their homework books.

Relaxation

For this relaxation activity, you need to pair the children up. In pairs, they then sit back-to-back and their task is to focus on how their partner is breathing. They have got to focus really hard to try and hear how their partner is breathing (e.g. loud, fast, or deep, etc.), and also to feel how their body is moving as they breathe in and out (e.g. up and down, forwards and backwards, etc.). They can do this while relaxing music is playing in the background and can then share what they noticed about their partner's breathing with the other children, at the end of the activity.

Resources

- Settling-down poem and music (if needed)
- Scenarios and choices on individual pieces of paper
- Large red circles and green hearts cut out from card
- Two bean bags
- Scissors and glue
- Pens and pencils
- Small red circles and green hearts cut out from card
- Relaxing music
- Homework books

Homework

Give the children some extra green hearts and red circles for them to take home. They can then spend some time at home talking to their family and looking through picture books, to identify the effects that positive and negative choices have on others around them. They can then record positive effects on green hearts as drawings and words, and negative effects on red circles, which they can then stick into their homework books.

Session 8

Learning objective

- I know how to show others I care about them

Settling-down poem

> 'Here are my ears, I can hear,
> Here are my eyes, I can see,
> Here is my heart, I can feel,
> Here is my friend, next to me,
> I am ready to learn and play,
> I'm sitting down, legs crossed, hooray!'

Warm-up game

The children will be able to play the 'Pass the clothes' game by using a bag of silly clothes (e.g. silly hat, silly shoes, silly glasses, etc.), and some fast-paced music. The children sit in a circle and pass the bag around while the music is playing, but as soon as the music stops, whomever is holding the bag needs to pick out a clothes item and put it on. The music then starts again and the bag is passed around once more until it stops and another item of clothing is taken out. Keep playing this game until either all of the children have had an opportunity to put some silly clothes on, or you run out of clothes.

Main activity

For this activity, you and the children will be creating 'Caring Windmill Flowers'. Before the start of the session, you will need to find a simple flower outline with four or five petals that you can photocopy for all the children to have one each. The first part of the activity will involve you and the children looking through different picture books to try and find examples of how you can show others that you care about them. When you have found one example, the children can record this as a drawing on one of their flower petals and you can then label it for them. You can then continue to look through the books and find more examples that the children can add to their flowers. Once all of their flower petals are full, they can then colour them in and cut out the flower. Using straws and split pins, you can then help the children to make a windmill by pushing the pin through the middle of the flower and then through the straw; you may need to make some cuts in the straw with a scissors before the start of the session.

Relaxation

Using the flower windmills that the children have made in the previous activity, they can practise their deep breathing. They need to take deep breaths in and then breathe out deeply in order to try and make their flower move. In order to see what works best and what makes them feel calmer, they can try and do this while they are standing, then sitting, and then lying on the floor, while relaxing music is playing in the background.

Resources

- Settling-down poem and music (if needed)
- Bag of silly clothes
- Fast-paced music
- Lots of picture books
- Flower outlines
- Coloured pencils, crayons, and pens
- Scissors, split pins, and straws
- Relaxing music
- Homework books

Homework

The children can take their windmill flowers home so that they can remember what they did during the main activity. Their homework activity could either involve them making a second flower windmill at home, or drawing a large flower outline in their homework books. Their task is to then observe others around them and to look through books to see if they can spot other examples of what other people can do to show that they care. With support, they can then draw what they find on individual flower petals, and then label what they have drawn.

Section 6 – Learning

From a young age, children use their senses to explore and make sense of their environment; they learn by watching and listening to others, although they acquire more knowledge and skills by doing things. They therefore learn best from being active participants that engage in play and practical activities that support the development of their language, their thinking skills, and their imagination. Children learn at a different pace to their peers but they all benefit from learning within an environment that offers them stimulating opportunities to engage and play, as well as a place where they feel nurtured, safe, and loved.

Learning is not just about progress and achievements that are academically focused, but encompasses skills that are part of a child's overall development. A child's ability to learn about who they are and to feel good about themselves is an integral part of their emotional growth, which leads to increased levels of confidence that empowers them to explore their world, take risks, and cope when things do not go as they wish. They also learn about how to build connections with others and to engage in positive interactions with those around them, which supports their social skills and communication. Part of responding to others and being part of society is their ability to learn about their feelings, and how these coupled with their thoughts can lead to actions and behaviours that will affect them and others that are part of their world.

Young children are able to take in a range of information from all around them at the same time, and can then start to make connections between different experiences that they encounter. Even if these experiences are not related in any way, children still have the ability to connect them in a meaningful way, which demonstrates creativity and flexible thinking. Children are curious and have a range of different ideas that they want to explore, which leads to them being flexible about what they think and how they act. This flexibility and ability to use their imagination helps them to test out theories that they have created about situations and the world around them. The act of testing out their thoughts by doing, and trial-and-error, allows them to make decisions, to try and solve problems, and to overcome difficult situations, which supports the development of their independence, their confidence, their ability to cope, and thus their resilience.

The ability to investigate their theories, plan how to do things, and then modify what they are going to do next according to what they now know, is linked to children's executive functioning. Executive functions enable children to manage themselves and their inner resources in order to achieve a goal; this involves mental manipulation and organisation of information, self-regulation, the ability to monitor one's performance, and to respond appropriately to situations. Furthermore, this involves metacognitive skills since being aware of the way that they think is needed to support the monitoring, organisation, processing, and adaptation of information during tasks. Metacognition also involves a child's ability to reflect on what they have done and to then choose different strategies to help them to carry out a task differently, which makes it a significant factor that contributes to successful learning.

As children grow, they benefit from being given constructive feedback so that they are able to reflect on their actions and their decisions; this helps them to keep learning about themselves and to take responsibility for their choices. This includes being aware of their strengths and the areas that require improvements, which involves considering that making mistakes is a way of learning something new or an opportunity to make something better. This implies that we can keep adapting and building our knowledge and skills since learning and achievement is not fixed; this is the core belief of having a growth mindset. It is important for children to understand as early as possible that they have the power to develop their skills and talents through perseverance and hard work, rather than believing that their level of intelligence and therefore potential, is fixed.

The activities within this programme that aim to support the development of learning skills focus on working with children so that they begin to recognise what they are good at, and then how to use this knowledge to help them through challenges and tricky times. Part of the learning journey is to help the children consider what they need to do in order to work in a group, and then how to tell others around them when they need or want something, of which a vital element is being able to ask relevant people for help. The activities also include opportunities for the children to begin to develop their awareness of the need to persevere and adopt an early growth mindset by reflecting on what they can do to keep going when things are hard, as well as identifying what they would like to get better at doing. This includes the ability to realise that mistakes are not failures, but rather, opportunities to make something better or try something in a new way.

Session 1

Learning objective

- I know what I am good at

Settling-down poem

> 'Here are my ears, I can hear,
> Here are my eyes, I can see,
> Here is my heart, I can feel,
> Here is my friend, next to me,
> I am ready to learn and play,
> I'm sitting down, legs crossed, hooray!'

Warm-up game

Play a circle game with the children called 'Wake up, wake up!' where one child sits in the centre of the circle and pretends to be asleep while a noisy toy (e.g. jingle bells or a set of keys) is placed in front of them. One child in the circle is then chosen to go and take the toy without making any noise, and to then sit back in their space while hiding the toy. The group then calls out 'wake up, wake up' for the child in the middle to wake up and guess who has taken the toy. When the toy has been found, the child who has hidden it then gets the opportunity to be the sleepy one in the centre of the circle. Play along until all of the children are able to have a go at being the one asleep in the middle.

Main activity

Before the session starts, find pictures of children doing different things (e.g. playing football, drawing, running, reading, helping, building, etc.), and have them ready for the activity.

Place all the pictures that you have found in front of the children and then give each child a tray. The children then look at all the pictures and pick up the ones that show what they are good at, which they then get to keep in their own tray. If there are children that want the same picture, either have several copies of each picture, or allow those children to sit next to each other and share the picture. They can then each have a turn to show the group what pictures they have in their tray and tell everyone what they are good at.

An extension of this activity is to enable the children to give each other pictures of things that they think another child in the group is good at. Have all the pictures in front of the children again and then ask each one to go and pick a picture of something that they think one of their peers is good at, and then place this picture in their peer's tray.

Relaxation

This activity is for the children to pass around a warm feeling. Ask the first child to rub their hands together until they begin to feel warm, and then pass this warm feeling on to the child sitting next to them by placing their hands together. After one round of this, the children then repeat passing around a warm feeling, but this time accompanied by a smile. The third round should extend this so that the children pass round the warm feeling, smile, and then lay on the floor with their eyes closed. Then let the children spend a few minutes with their eyes closed, listening to some relaxing and calm music.

Resources

- Settling-down poem and music (if needed)
- Noisy toy (e.g. jingle bells, set of keys, etc.)
- Pictures of children doing different things
- A small tray for each child
- Relaxing music
- Homework books

Homework

In their homework books, the children need to work with an adult to draw pictures of what they are good at, or cut out and stick in pictures that they have cut out from old magazines representing what they are good at. If possible, they could also stick in photographs of themselves doing what they are good at, if they have these available.

Session 2

Learning objective

- I know how to use what I am good at to help me

Settling-down poem

> 'Here are my ears, I can hear,
> Here are my eyes, I can see,
> Here is my heart, I can feel,
> Here is my friend, next to me,
> I am ready to learn and play,
> I'm sitting down, legs crossed, hooray!'

Warm-up game

Play the 'Copy Me' game with the children where you start off modelling some actions and they have to observe you carefully and then copy what you do. Once you have done a few actions with them, give each child the opportunity to be the leader who models the actions, and you and the other children have to copy them.

Main activity

For this activity, you will need the pictures that you used in the previous session when you looked at what the children are good at, and it may also be useful to look back in their homework books and find the pages where they further recorded what they feel they are good at. You will also need coloured rectangular pieces of paper to represent bricks, and large pieces of sugar paper on which to stick these. Give each child several pieces of these rectangular pieces of paper, but of the same colour so that each child has bricks of only one colour. Ask the children to refer back to the pictures and homework from the previous session, and to record one thing that they are good at on separate rectangles, as drawings or words. Once they have done this, each child gets their own large piece of sugar paper on which to stick down their rectangular pieces of paper to resemble beginning to build a wall with individual bricks. Since this concept is not an easy one, the next part of this activity will require adult support in order to help the children think of ways that their strengths can help them in areas that they might find more tricky. You can work on this as a group by looking at one strength from each child and seeing how this could help them with something that they find hard to do. Examples of these might be:

- If you're good at building, you can use that to help you with your learning, such as building up words or with counting.
- If you're good at helping, you can help someone when they need it and then they can help you when you need it.
- If you're good at drawing, you can draw what you know or what you want to express, if you find it hard to write it in words or say it.
- If you're good at talking, you can ask someone for help or you can explain what you are finding difficult.
- If you're good at running, you can run around fast when you are finding it hard to cope because you feel angry.

When you have worked out how one of their strengths can help them with other areas, the children then need to record this. Have different paper shapes available (e.g. of flowers, hearts, or stars, etc.); the children can choose what shape to use to record how one of their strengths can help them, in words or as a drawing. When they have done this, they can stick this shape down on their brick wall. If you have time, you can choose another strength for each child and work out how this could help them with areas of difficulty, and again encourage them to record this on a paper shape that gets stuck to their wall. Make sure to help the children to label the drawings on their paper shapes so that everyone knows what they have drawn.

Relaxation

Before the start of the session, you will need to prepare the following: use one large piece of sugar paper per child and on each piece, draw long and squiggly interwoven lines in four different colours all over the page. Then, get some small pom-pom balls or counters in the same four colours in which you have drawn the coloured lines.

For this activity, give each child one sheet of sugar paper with the coloured lines and four colour-corresponding pom-pom balls or counters, and their task is to slowly and carefully follow each line with its corresponding colour ball or counter, making sure to follow it all the way around. They should only be focusing on doing this quietly, as calm and relaxing music plays in the background.

Resources

- Settling-down poem and music (if needed)
- Pictures from the previous session
- Paper shapes (e.g. hearts, stars) and rectangular pieces of paper in different colours

- Glue sticks
- Pens and pencils
- Large pieces of sugar paper for each child and markers of four different colours
- Craft pom-pom balls or counters of four different colours
- Relaxing music
- Homework books

Homework

Get the children to take home the large pieces of sugar paper where they have begun to build their strengths wall, and to take more rectangular pieces of paper for their bricks and different paper shapes for their strategies to support areas of difficulty. They can carry on this activity at home with their parents so that they can continue to build their wall, and continue to work out ways that their strengths can help them. This activity can be added to over time, giving the children enough time to record the things that they can do well, alongside ideas of how these strengths can help them.

Session 3

Learning objective

- I know how to work in a group

Settling-down poem

'Here are my ears, I can hear,
Here are my eyes, I can see,
Here is my heart, I can feel,
Here is my friend, next to me,
I am ready to learn and play,
I'm sitting down, legs crossed, hooray!'

Warm-up game

The aim of this game is for the children to get from one side of the room to the other in pairs, but with a presenting obstacle. Each pair needs to be given a physical challenge such as holding a bean bag between their heads, a pillow between their backs, or a box between their bellies, and they then have to try to get to the other side of the room without dropping it.

Main activity

Have a variety of pictures available that show children working together in a group and demonstrating skills for effective group working, such as sharing, turn-taking, listening to each other, working together, sitting together, talking with each other, letting everyone have a go, helping each other, etc. Lay these pictures out on the floor for the children to see, and next to each picture, place a bowl or cup full of counters of one particular colour (for example: next to the picture of 'sharing' place a cup full of yellow counters and next to the picture of 'turn-taking' place a cup full of blue counters). The children have their own empty cup and walk around to look at all of the pictures; if they think that they do have the skill shown on a specific picture, they pick up a counter from that picture and put it in their own cup.

Once all of the children have seen all of the pictures and collected the counters relevant to them, they sit down together and share what counters they have collected that show how they are able to work well in a group. They can then collect more counters from each picture but have to give them out to their friends to express that they have noticed how their friends are also able to work well in a group.

Relaxation

You will need to model this exercise for the children so that they can hear and see what they need to do. Ask the children to imagine that they are standing on a beach on a very hot day, with the strong sun beating down on them. Explain that the sun is so strong that they can feel themselves begin to melt, like a ball of ice-cream melting on the floor. They can feel their fingers and toes getting heavier and heavier. Their body is relaxing and getting heavier and heavier until their skin and bones feel so heavy that they begin to droop downwards, closer to the ground. Their head feels heavier and begins to drop to the side, and then round to the front of their bodies. It feels as if they have no bones in their bodies, and so their skin and muscles begin to slowly melt towards the floor. They keep on melting, melting, melting, and melting slowly, until they are lying on the floor, sprawled out and enjoying feeling relaxed. They close their eyes and imagine lying on a warm beach, listening to the sound of the sea, and eating their favourite ice-cream. After around a minute or so, tell the children to open their eyes and sit back up when they are ready.

Resources

- Settling-down poem and music (if needed)
- Bean bags, boxes, pillows or cushions, etc. for the warm-up game
- Variety of pictures showing effective group-working skills
- Cups or bowls
- Coloured counters
- Homework books

Homework

Allow the children to take home the counters that they collected in the main activity. For homework, they need to draw around each of these counters in their books and colour them in to record how many they collected. With the support of an adult, they can then try and recall what picture (or skill) each coloured counter stood for, and then to draw a picture of this in their books as well. The adult can then write down what the child has drawn next to each picture, and they can then check whether the child is also able to use these skills at home (e.g. during meal times, playing with family or friends, doing chores, etc.).

Session 4

Learning objective

- I know how to tell others when I need or want something

Settling-down poem

> 'Here are my ears, I can hear,
> Here are my eyes, I can see,
> Here is my heart, I can feel,
> Here is my friend, next to me,
> I am ready to learn and play,
> I'm sitting down, legs crossed, hooray!'

Warm-up game

Show the children a colourful scarf and then ask them to close their eyes because you are going to hide it somewhere around the room. You then hide it but with a little corner sticking out so that it can be seen by careful observers! Ask the children to open their eyes and look around but without touching anything. When a child spots the scarf, they have to shout out 'Hooray!' but not to take it or point to the scarf so that the other children have to keep looking for it. The game carries on until everyone has spotted it and shouted 'Hooray!' Play a few rounds of this by hiding the scarf in different places, making it harder to spot each time you start a new round.

Main activity

This activity has three parts to it:

- First: when might you need to tell someone you need or want something?
- Second: who can you tell when you need or want something?
- Third: how can you tell someone when you need or want something?

Start off this activity by asking the children when they might need to tell someone that they need or want something, at school and at home. Examples of these could include:

- Asking for help when you cannot reach the cupboard door.
- When you need to get something but cannot find it.

78   Learning

- When you are feeling hungry.
- When you do not feel safe.
- When you can't see your Mum in the shop.

Then, give each child a large piece of sugar paper and some coloured markers. Ask the children who they can tell when they need or want something. This might include their parents, siblings, teachers, friends, and safe adults (e.g. a policeman). For each person that they can think of, they need to draw around one of their hands, and then inside each hand, they draw a picture of who that hand represents (e.g. one hand representing Dad and another representing Mum, another hand representing the teacher or a friend, etc.).

Once the children have drawn their hands and who those hands represent, ask them how they could tell these people when they needed or wanted something. These strategies might include talking to them, drawing for them, finding a picture to show what they might need or want, taking them and showing them what they need, etc. Have lots of old magazines available and ask the children to look through them and find pictures that show the different ways that they could let others know that they might need or want something. When they have found these, they can cut them out and stick them around the hands that they have drawn on their large piece of paper.

Relaxation

This activity aims to incorporate a mindfulness technique, which teaches the children to stop and focus on what is going on around them, without talking to each other. If possible, it is best to do this outside where the children can sit down in the fresh air and take in their surroundings. Ask the children to sit down and not to say anything, but quietly focus on what they can see around them. Then, ask them to close their eyes and focus on what they can hear around them. They can then take off their shoes (if possible) and walk around; focusing on how the ground beneath them feels. They can also move around quietly and touch objects around them, focusing on how they feel to the touch.

Resources

- Settling-down poem and music (if needed)
- Colourful scarf
- Large pieces of sugar paper
- Coloured markers
- Old magazines
- Scissors and glue sticks
- Homework books

Learning

Homework

Let the children take home the large pieces of paper from the main activity, and ask them to add on to what they have already done to include more hands for people that will be able to help them outside of school (e.g. grandparents, doctor, shopkeeper, nanny, etc.), and to include more ways that they can let them know what they need and want (for example: visiting them, writing them a letter, phoning them, etc.). The children can then record these ways of communicating as pictures that have been cut out from magazines, or as their own drawings.

Session 5

Learning objective

- I know how to ask for help

Settling-down poem

> 'Here are my ears, I can hear,
> Here are my eyes, I can see,
> Here is my heart, I can feel,
> Here is my friend, next to me,

*I am ready to learn and play,
I'm sitting down, legs crossed, hooray!'*

Warm-up game

Have a collection of around 12 random objects, a large tray on which to display them, and a blanket. Start with a small number of objects such as four items to introduce the children to the game; place these four objects in the tray, give the children around 30 seconds to look at them, then cover them with a blanket and ask the children to close their eyes. When they close their eyes, remove one object from under the blanket and hide it. Then tell the children to open their eyes, remove the blanket, and ask them to identify which object is missing. Keep making this activity harder by placing more objects on the tray, giving the children less time to look at the objects, or removing more than one item at a time for them to guess which are missing.

Main activity

Have a variety of materials available that will help you and the children build a den in the classroom, such as cushions, table cloths, blankets, etc. You could use tables and chairs to prop up the materials so that the den is big enough for one child to sit comfortably in, and make sure that you create a way for the children to get in and out of it. Each child then gets a turn to go and sit inside, and they then need to call out to the group and ask for help in order to be able to leave the den. The group outside need to decide whether what the child inside has said is enough to indicate that they need help, and if so, they can help them get out by saying 'Okay, we'll help'. If they feel that the child has not asked in the clearest way that shows that they need help, they then say 'Please try again'. Examples of what the children might successfully say are:

- I need help please.
- Help me get out please.
- Can you help me please?
- Can someone let me out please?
- I can't get out, help please.

Some examples of the things that they might say that is not a clear request for help are:

- I want to go.
- Open the door.
- Let me out.
- This is fun.
- I'm coming out.

Relaxation

Make the den from the previous session large enough so that there is a space for all the children to sit inside. Have a number of objects that light up available such as a torch, a light-up wand, a rotating light-up wand, and light-up squeezy toys. Make sure that the den is dark and then switch every light source on individually and move it around the den so that the children can watch the patterns around them. They need to sit quietly and watch the lights as they listen to relaxing music being played in the background.

Resources

- Settling-down poem and music (if needed)
- 12 random objects
- Large tray
- Blanket
- Den-building materials (e.g. blankets, cushions, tablecloths)
- Light-up toys
- Relaxing music
- Homework books

Homework

At home, the children need to become 'Help Detectives' where they have to watch others around them and spot when they have asked someone for help. When they spot someone asking for help, with support they need to record what they have noticed in their homework books using drawings and word captions. The children need to try and spot as many different ways as they can of asking for help, and to record (e.g. as ticks or crosses) the amount of times that they have seen one type of asking for help (e.g. someone saying 'Help me please').

Session 6

Learning objective

- I know how to keep going when things are hard

Settling-down poem

'Here are my ears, I can hear,
Here are my eyes, I can see,
Here is my heart, I can feel,
Here is my friend, next to me,
I am ready to learn and play,
I'm sitting down, legs crossed, hooray!'

82 Learning

Warm-up game

Before the start of the session, gather two large-piece puzzles that are age-appropriate for the children you are working with. Pull out the pieces and hide them in different places around the room. When the children start the activity, show them the two pictures for each of the puzzles and tell them that you have lost the pieces all around the room. Ask them to go on a hunt for the puzzle pieces and once they have found one, they have to find the other children who will have pieces for the same puzzle as the one that they have found. They then have to check whether they can already connect the pieces that they have found, and once they have put the pieces together, they can then go off to try and find even more.

Main activity

Find two story books that focus on the need to keep going, even when things get tough. Two lovely books that have this as their main theme are *The Most Magnificent Thing* by Ashley Spires, and *The Little Engine That Could* by Pseud Piper Watty. If you are not able to get copies of these books, video clips of them being read can be found on YouTube. Gather some coloured A4 card pieces and cut these in half so that you have smaller rectangles, and also cut out small black circles.

Read the two stories mentioned above to the children; the activity can then focus on a positive statement that was emphasised in the story of *The Little Engine That Could*, which states 'I think I can, I think I can'. Use one A4 piece of card and draw a simple outline for a train engine and inside it write the words 'I think I can, I think I can'. Then, give each child a smaller rectangle card piece and tell them that together you can think of things that they might find hard but which they will be able to tackle when they think that they can do it and persevere. Ask each child what they find hard or what they want to get better at, and they can draw a picture of this on their piece of card. You can then label their picture as an 'I think I can ...' statement, for example:

- If a child finds writing his name hard, the caption could read 'I think I can write my name' or 'I think I can learn to write my name'.
- If a child finds sitting still hard, the caption could read 'I think I can sit still'.
- If a child finds it hard to ride her bicycle, the caption could read 'I think I can ride my bicycle' or 'I think I can learn to ride my bicycle'.

When you and the children have done this, you can then begin sticking their rectangles together in a line to form the train carriages, and then attaching these to the engine that you drew so that you can build your very own 'I think I can' train. Do not forget to add the small black cardboard circles to your train that will be the wheels for each of the carriages. Check to see if the children have any other ideas of what they find hard that they might want to draw on pieces of card and add to the train.

Relaxation

The children will be able to practise the art of 'stretchy cat, hidden turtle' by listening to you as you describe the relaxation exercise below, and following your actions to help them.

- Pretend you are a cat asleep on the floor. You are curled up into a ball, snoozing away in a soft spot, breathing in through your mouth and breathing out through your nose as you sleep. Breathe in again slowly through your mouth and breathe out slowly through your nose. Breathe in slowly and breathe out slowly. You feel so relaxed and sleepy.
- Suddenly you hear a sound and your eyes open slowly. You stretch out your arms and your legs, stretching them out as wide as you can. Your fingers and toes are now kitty claws and you curl up your fingers and toes, squeezing them as tight as you can. Keep squeezing tight, a bit tighter, and a little bit tighter. Now relax those claws little kitty. Stretch your fingers and toes as much as you can and feel them relax.
- Now you let out one big yawn and stand up on your knees and hands, like a kitty ready to go for a walk. You look down and suddenly, you've turned into a turtle! You slowly, very slowly start walking forward, breathing in through your mouth and breathing out through your nose. Breathing in slowly and breathing out slowly. You feel very tired again so you move your shoulders up and push your head down into your neck. You hold your head down tight for a little while and then stretch it out as much as you can. You give a great big yawn and then curl up on the floor with your head tucked into your arms. You feel very snoozy and fall asleep just as you are, breathing in slowly through your mouth and breathing out slowly through your nose. Breathing in slowly and breathing out slowly. Goodnight little turtle . . .

Resources

- Settling-down poem and music (if needed)
- 'The most magnificent thing' picture book or video clip
- 'The little engine that could' picture book or video clip
- One large piece of coloured card
- Small pieces of coloured card (e.g. A4 pieces cut in half)
- Small black cardboard circles
- Sticky tape
- Homework books

84 Learning

Homework

Give the children some extra rectangular pieces of card for them to take home so that they can continue to draw pictures of what they find hard. With support, the children can think of different things that they find hard at school and at home, and then draw pictures of these on individual pieces of card. They can then get some help from their family to label their drawings with sentences that start as 'I think I can ...'. The children can then bring these pieces of card to school and add them to the train that you created as a group during the main activity.

Session 7

Learning objective

- I know what I want to get better at

Settling-down poem

'Here are my ears, I can hear,
Here are my eyes, I can see,
Here is my heart, I can feel,
Here is my friend, next to me,
I am ready to learn and play,
I'm sitting down, legs crossed, hooray!'

Warm-up game

Have a container full of coloured counters or small coloured objects available for the children to use, such as unifix cubes or counting bears. Ask each of them to reach in and take one of the objects and then give them 30 seconds to wander around the room and collect as many items as they can find that are the same colour. After 30 seconds, ask them to come back to you and place what they have found in individual bags or containers, and then ask them to pick out another colour and give them the same amount of time to collect more items. Allow the children to do this a number of times and then ask them to count how many items they have collected in their bag or container; the winner is the one who has gathered the most items and who could then win a prize such as a sticker or small stationery item.

Main activity

Try and find a picture book about using bricks to build something such as *Billions of Bricks* by Kurt Cyrus. You will also need lots of brick-shaped pieces of paper or card for the children to use during this activity.

Read the story you have found to the children and highlight that a wall is part of something bigger, giving it shape and making it stronger, like a house.

Explain to them that people have lots of things that they are good at or that they would like to get better at, which will help them create lots of things and make them stronger in what they do (like a wall). Ask each child to name one thing that they would like to get better at and then tell them to record this as a drawing on a brick-shaped piece of card, which you can then label for them. Encourage the children to think of as many things as they can that they would like to get better at doing at school and at home, and to record all of these on individual brick-shaped cards. You and the children can then start sticking these bricks down on a large piece of card so that you can start building your own 'Skills Wall'.

An extension to this activity is to have some cardboard shapes available such as stars or flowers so that you and the children can record what kind of things they might need to do to help them get better at what they have identified as an area that they would like to develop. For example, if they identified that they want to get better at reading, what they would need to do is to 'read with my teacher every day', or if they want to get better at riding their bicycle, they would need to 'practise cycling in the garden'. These shapes can then be stuck on the 'Skills Wall' as strategies that can be implemented to support them to develop their skills.

Relaxation

Before the session, you can create some cornflour and water mixture that the children will love playing with. This mixture produces a substance that is both solid and liquid at the same time, which will be fascinating for the children to watch and use as a relaxing activity.

Make sure that you make enough mixture so that there is enough for each child to have their own container to play with. For example, use a bowl for each child where you place an equal amount (e.g. a cup) of cornflour and water, mix it well, and then add some food colouring to make it colourful. The children can then sit on the floor and play with their mixture, sifting it with their hands, moving their fingers through it, and focusing on how it feels. They can do this while practising their deep breathing, being role-modelled by you, while listening to relaxing music.

Resources

- Settling-down poem and music (if needed)
- Container with small coloured objects (e.g. unifix cubes, counting bears, etc.)
- One bag or container for each child
- Prizes such as stickers
- Picture book about using bricks for building
- Large piece of card
- Brick-shaped pieces of paper or card

86   Learning

- Small pieces of card such as flowers or star shapes
- Pens and pencils
- Glue sticks
- Cornflour, water, and food colouring
- Individual bowls for each child
- Relaxing music
- Homework books

Homework

Give the children some extra brick-shaped cards and smaller card shapes such as flowers to take home. For homework, they need to work with their family to think of more things that they would like to get better at, which they can record as drawings on individual brick shapes. With support they can then label what their drawings represent and then think about what they will need to do to get better at what they have identified, which can be recorded on the smaller card shapes. The children can then bring these shapes into school and add them to the 'Skills Wall' that they started to build during the main activity.

Session 8

Learning objective

- I know it's okay to make mistakes

Settling-down poem

> 'Here are my ears, I can hear,
> Here are my eyes, I can see,
> Here is my heart, I can feel,
> Here is my friend, next to me,
> I am ready to learn and play,
> I'm sitting down, legs crossed, hooray!'

Warm-up game

This warm-up activity should be free-choice where the children can choose what they want to do. Look over all of the previous sessions and pick five warm-up activities that you think the children have really enjoyed doing, as well as gather all the resources that you may need for any of these five games. The children can then vote and choose what activity out of the five they would like to do and if there is time, they could even choose a second activity from the five offered.

Main activity

This activity needs a picture book that focuses on how it is alright to make mistakes, such as *Beautiful Oops* by Barney Saltzberg, and *It's Okay to Make*

Mistakes by Todd Parr. Both of these stories can be found as YouTube clips online if you are not able to get hold of the picture books for the session. Read these stories to the children and highlight how the main element to these stories is how it is okay to make mistakes as they let us create different things, learn better, and make amends. Give each child a small piece of paper and ask them to draw a picture of a mistake that they have made, and then colour it in. When the children show their drawings and explain what they are, get them to think about how that mistake is okay to make, in the same way that the mistakes in the stories turned out even better than expected. These drawings can then be glued on to a large piece of card that you as a group can turn into a poster called 'Oops and Uh-Ohs, Helps Us Grow'. Give the children time to add as many individual drawings to the poster as possible and to then decorate it with lots of different colours and craft materials. This can then become a visual poster of how it is okay to make lots of mistakes, and as a reminder that mistakes should not stop you from doing anything.

Relaxation

Before the start of the session, cut out a large circle from a large piece of card and divide it into eight sections. Look through all of the relaxation activities from the previous sessions and choose eight that you know that the children enjoyed doing, as well as the ones that helped to make them feel calmer and more relaxed. On each of the eight sections of the circle, write a word and add a simple picture or symbol to represent what relaxation activity it stands for. Then, cut a large thin arrow from the same piece of card, punch a hole in the end, and using a split-pin, attach the arrow to the circle so that you create a spinning wheel. Make sure that you also gather all the resources that you will need for each of these eight activities.

Lay this spinning wheel on the floor and give one child a turn at spinning the arrow to see where it lands. The group then engage in whichever activity the arrow has landed on, and then move on to the next activity when a second child has had an opportunity to spin the wheel. Make sure that all the children have a chance to spin the wheel and choose a relaxation activity for everyone to engage in.

Resources
- Settling-down poem and music (if needed)
- Resources for five warm-up activities chosen for this session
- Picture books about making mistakes
- Small pieces of card
- Large piece of card
- Pens, pencils, and markers
- Glue stick

88   Learning

- Craft materials such as glitter, tissues paper, gems, etc.
- Large piece of card for the spinning wheel
- Split-pin and hole punch
- Scissors
- Resources for eight chosen relaxation activities
- Homework books

Homework

Take a photograph of the 'Oops and Uh-Ohs, Helps Us Grow' poster that you and the children have created and then print out a copy for every child. Glue these copies into their homework books so that their family can see what they have been doing in the session. Their homework is to then work with their family to create their own 'Oops and Uh-Ohs, Helps Us Grow' posters for them to put up at home, as visual reminders that it is okay to make mistakes.

Appendices

Learning Objectives Table

Core Area	Objective
Relationships	I know what a good friend is I know that I am a good friend I know who my friends are and why I know who is in my family I know how to make friends I know how to keep my friends I know what I like doing with my friends I know how to do something kind for others
Emotions	I know when I feel happy or sad I know when others feel happy or sad I know what makes me and others feel happy I know what makes me and others feel sad I know when I am feeling angry I know what makes me feel angry I know how to make myself feel better I know how to make others feel better
Awareness	I know things about me such as what I look like I know what is special about me I know what I like and what I don't like I know how we are the same and different I know that I can make good choices I know what to do if I haven't made a good choice I know how my choices can affect others I know how to show others I care about them
Learning	I know what I am good at I know how to use what I am good at to help me I know how to work in a group I know how to tell others when I need or want something I know how to ask for help I know how to keep going when things are hard I know what I want to get better at I know it's okay to make mistakes

Homework Activities Table

Relationships Session 1 – I know what a good friend is

The children have been working on recognising the qualities of a good friend. With the help of an adult at home, the children need to look through a few of their story books to try and find examples of when they can spot the story characters being good friends to each other. They can then choose one or a few of these examples and draw pictures of them in their homework books, which the supporting adult can then help them to label or caption.

Relationships Session 2 – I know that I am a good friend

The children need to look back at the pictures that they have drawn in their books of characters that they had found in stories showing qualities of good friends. They can then draw a smiley face or a tick next to each drawing if they feel that they are also a good friend in the same way as is depicted in the drawing. If they remember other qualities that make them a good friend that they have not yet drawn, they can draw these in their books too.

Relationships Session 3 – I know who my friends are and why

The children have been drawing pictures of their friends. They can talk to an adult about them and what they feel is each friend's best friendship quality. They can then think about other people around them (their family) and think about whether they can notice these characteristics in them too. If so, the children can draw pictures of those people and the supporting adult can note down the quality the child has chosen to describe them.

Relationships Session 4 – I know who is in my family

The children have been sticking pictures of people that could be different family members into their books. At home, an adult can label these pictures for them or they can have a go at writing the words themselves. Their homework is to then collect photographs of their family and stick these into their books, and with support if needed, label who everyone is.

Relationships Session 5 – I know how to make friends

The children have been creating a poster at school and a photograph of this poster has been stuck into their books. The children can therefore use this photograph as an example of a friendship poster that they can create at home. They can take their time to make their own posters with their family at home, and then if possible, take a photograph of what they have created and also stick this into their homework books to share with others at school.

Relationships Session 6 – I know how to keep my friends

The children need to draw around their hands several times in their books and take it round to their family members to ask them what they do to keep their friends. With help, these things can be recorded on each of the hands that they have drawn, as drawings or words.

Relationships Session 7 – I know what I like doing with my friends

The children have been sticking pictures in their books of things that they like doing with their friends. For homework, they have to find more pictures (e.g. cut out from old magazines) that they can stick into their homework books, or do some drawings of other things that they also like doing with their friends.

Relationship Session 8 – I know how to do something kind for others

The children have stuck into their homework books a picture of something kind that they would like to do for someone else. Their homework is to look through old magazines or newspapers at home to find more kindness pictures, cut these out, and then stick them in their books. With support, they can then label who they will be doing these acts of kindness for, and they can then start doing these acts for the people that they have chosen.

Emotions Session 1 – I know when I feel happy or sad

The children are taking yellow and blue pom-poms or counters home that they have been using at school, and they need to stick these in their books. With support from an adult, they then draw pictures and write words for each of them to show what they represent in terms of what they do when they are feeling happy and sad. Yellow pom-poms or counters should represent how the children act when they are feeling happy, and the blue pom-poms or counters should represent how the children act when they are feeling sad.

Emotions Session 2 – I know when others feel happy or sad

Since the last homework session was for the children to draw pictures and with support write words to represent the yellow and blue pom-poms showing happy and sad behaviours, this session's homework is for them to try and observe these behaviours in others around them. They can then place a tick or mark of their choosing next to each pom-pom, depending on what happy and sad behaviours they notice in their family, friends, and out in their community.

Emotions Session 3 – I know what makes me and others feel happy

The children need to find one picture from an old magazine of someone feeling happy. They then cut this out and stick it on to a blank page in their homework books. The children will need to think of things that make them feel happy and will need to record these on the page with the happy picture. They can choose to cut out more pictures from magazines or draw pictures of the things that make them feel happy.

Emotions Session 4 – I know what makes me and others feel sad

The children need to find one picture from a magazine of someone feeling sad. They then cut this out and stick it on to a blank page in their homework books. The children will need to think of things that make them feel sad and will need to record these on the page with the sad picture. They can choose to cut out more pictures from magazines or draw pictures of the things that make them feel sad.

Emotions Session 5 – I know when I am feeling angry

With adult support, the children need to draw an outline of a body in their homework books and then, with coloured pens, draw or colour in the parts of the body that change when they start feeling angry, just as they have done in the session at school. If they become angry before the next session, they then need to record in their books what happened or what made them feel angry, so that they can then share this with the group in the next session.

Emotions Session 6 – I know what makes me feel angry

In their homework books, the children need to draw pictures of the things that they know make them feel angry. They will also need to extend this by observing those around them and recording what they have noticed that makes others feel angry.

Emotions Session 7 – I know how to make myself feel better

The children are taking home a variety of colourful pieces of paper and with support from an adult, they need to explore ways that could be helpful in order to make them feel better (e.g. going for a walk, running around, having a sleep, etc.). They then record these as drawings and words on their individual pieces of paper, and then stick these into their homework books.

Emotions Session 8 – I know how to make others feel better

The children are taking home a variety of colourful pieces of paper so that they can ask their family members about ways that they find helpful to calm them down. They then record these as drawings and words, with support, on their individual pieces of paper. The children can then decide whether they want to stick their pieces of paper in their homework books or whether they want to take them in to school and place them in the 'Helpful Heroes' box. They could even create their own box at home with strategies that they have explored with their family and friends.

Awareness Session 1 – I know things about me such as what I look like

The children are taking home the 'All About Me' posters that they have started creating during the session at school, and they can then finish this with support from their family, for homework. They can also add photographs to their posters and decorate them in whichever way that they wish.

Awareness Session 2 – I know what is special about me

The children are taking home some small pieces of paper like the ones that they used during the session at school, so that they can draw pictures on each piece about the things that they feel make them special and unique. Their family can help them to do this task and they can then stick down the pictures in their homework books with labels or captions.

Awareness Session 3 – I know what I like and what I don't like

In their homework books, the children need to write or draw pictures of the things that they like and do not like when they are at home or away from school. They also need to spend some time with their family to find out what they like and do not like, and together they can also record these as drawings or words in their books. They can extend this activity by looking through books and trying to spot when characters express their likes and dislikes.

Awareness Session 4 – I know how we are the same and different

The children need to carry out an investigation at home with the help of a parent. They need to observe their family and friends carefully, and in their homework books note down in pictures or words, what similarities and differences that they can see in them (e.g. their hair and eye colour, height, clothes, what they like and do not like, etc.).

Awareness Session 5 – I know that I can make good choices

The children have drawn two pictures in their homework books of two puppets that were used in the session. With their family's support, they have to observe what others around them do, and try and work out if anything they saw was a positive or a negative choice. They can then record what they have noticed as drawings in their books, on whichever page corresponds to the puppet and choice that was made. The children will need some support to do this as a way of getting them to begin to notice the kinds of choices that others around them are making.

Awareness Session 6 – I know what to do if I haven't made a good choice

The children have to observe others around them and try and identify times when they have made the incorrect choice, and then try and identify what they did to make amends. This might be difficult for some of the children to spot so they could be supported to do this activity by sitting down with their parents and asking them when they have made a negative choice and what they did to make it better. The children can then draw pictures of these strategies in their homework books and with help, label what they have drawn.

Awareness Session 7 – I know how my choices can affect others

The children are taking home some small green hearts and red circles for their homework activity. They can then spend some time at home talking to their family and looking through picture books, to identify the effects that positive and negative choices have on others around them. They can then record positive effects on green hearts as drawings and words, and negative effects on red circles, which they can then stick into their homework books.

Awareness Session 8 – I know how to show others I care about them

The children are taking their windmill flowers home that they have created at school, so that they can remember what they did during the main activity. Their homework activity could either involve them making a second flower windmill at home, or drawing a large flower outline in their homework books. Their task is to then observe others around them and to look through books to see if they can spot other examples of what people can do to show that they care. With support, they can then draw what they find on individual flower petals, and then label what they have drawn.

Learning Session 1 – I know what I am good at

In their homework books, the children need to work with an adult to draw pictures of what they are good at, or stick in pictures that they have cut out from old magazines representing what they are good at. If possible, they could also stick in photographs of themselves doing what they are good at, if they have these available. An extension to this activity is to ask their family members what they feel they are good at, which they can also record in their books as drawings and words.

Learning Session 2 – I know how to use what I am good at to help me

The children are taking home large pieces of sugar paper where they have begun to build their strengths wall, and are also taking extra rectangular pieces of paper for their bricks and different paper shapes for their strategies to support areas of difficulty that they identify. They can carry on doing this activity at home with their family so that they can continue to build their wall, and continue to work out ways that their strengths can help them. On the bricks, they record examples of what they are good at, and on the paper shapes, they record how these things can help them to learn or accomplish other things.

Learning Session 3 – I know how to work in a group

The children are taking home counters that they collected in the activity at school. For homework, they need to draw around each of these counters in their books and colour them in to record how many they collected. With the support of an adult, they can then try and recall what picture (or skill) each coloured counter stood for, and then to draw a picture of this in their books as well. The adult can then write down what the child has drawn next to each picture, and they can then check whether the child is also able to use these skills at home (e.g. during meal times, playing with family or friends, doing chores, etc.).

Learning Session 4 – I know how to tell others when I need or want something

The children are taking home large pieces of paper from the activity at school, and they need to add on to what they have already done to include more hands for people that will be able to help them outside of school (e.g. grandparents, doctor, shopkeeper, nanny, etc.). They also need to include more ways that they can let people know what they need and want (e.g. visiting them, writing them a letter, phoning them, etc.). The children can then record these ways of communicating as pictures that have been cut out from magazines, or as their own drawings and words.

Learning Session 5 – I know how to ask for help

At home, the children need to become 'Help Detectives' where they have to watch others around them and spot when they have asked someone for help. When they spot someone asking for help, with support they need to record what they have noticed, in their homework books using drawings and word captions. The children need to try and spot as many different ways as they can of asking for help, and to record (e.g. as ticks or crosses) the amount of times that they have seen one type of asking for help (e.g. someone saying 'Help me please' or taking someone by the hand to show them what they need).

Learning Session 6 – I know how to keep going when things are hard

The children are taking home some extra rectangular pieces of card so that they can continue to draw pictures of what they find hard. With support from an adult, the children need to think of different things that they find hard at school and at home, and then draw pictures of these on individual pieces of card. They can then get some help from their family to label their drawings with positive sentences that start as 'I think I can ...' (e.g. I think I can ... learn to spell a new word). The children can then take these pieces of card to school and add them to the train that was created with their group during the main activity of the session.

Learning Session 7 – I know what I want to get better at

The children are taking some extra brick-shaped cards and smaller card shapes home such as flowers and stars. For homework, they need to work with their family to think of more things that they would like to get better at, which they can record as drawings on individual brick shapes. With support, they can then label what their drawings represent and then think about what they will need to do to get better at what they have identified, which can be recorded on the smaller card shapes. The children can then take these shapes into school and add them to the 'Skills Wall' that they started to build during the main activity of the session.

Learning Session 8 – I know it's okay to make mistakes

In their homework books, there is a photograph of an 'Oops and Uh-Ohs, Helps Us Grow' poster that the children have been creating at school. This lets their families see what they have been doing in the session. Their homework is to then work with their family to create their own 'Oops and Uh-Ohs, Helps Us Grow' posters for them to put up at home, which will serve as a visual reminder that it is okay to make mistakes.